I0817940
Pizza Planet

Pizza Planet

Disney · PIXAR

TOY STORY

THE Pizza Planet COOKBOOK

THE Pizza Planet COOKBOOK

OFFICIAL RECIPES FROM YOUR FAVORITE FOOD AND FUN SPACEPORT

Sarah Walker Caron

SAN RAFAEL • LOS ANGELES • LONDON

CHAPTER 1: WELCOME TO PIZZA PLANET

CHAPTER 2: EARTHLING FAVORITES (CLASSIC PIZZAS AND SANDWICHES)

MENU

CHAPTER 3: OUT-OF-THIS-WORLD SPECIALTY PIZZAS

CHAPTER 4: INTERSTELLAR SIDES AND SALADS

CHAPTER 5: STARRY SWEETS AND SIPS

EXTRAS

MENU

FUELING STATION
Pizza Planet
PIZZAS
SALADS
SNACKS
BEVERAGES
STAR CLUSTER
GET 1 FREE PIZZA
ORDER

Chapter 1

Welcome to PIZZA PLANET

THE PIZZA PLANET KITCHEN

Welcome! You've been cleared for entry into the inner workings of the spaceport, and we're thrilled to have you join us on the mission: to entertain and nourish our Pizza Planet visitors!

This handbook has been written to provide our intergalactic team members, aka Voyagers, with guidelines, tips, and advice to ensure all Pizza Planet guests have an out-of-this-world experience. Do us proud, Pizza Planet Voyager!

- **Company Mission:** We dedicate ourselves to making every Pizza Planet experience so memorable that our fans can't wait to return for another liftoff.

Tools and Ingredients You'll Find at Our Spaceport

If you're new to making pizza, it might seem like you need a lot of specialty equipment, but the truth is that having the right tools of the trade will ensure optimal pizza results every time.

TOOLS

- **16-inch (40cm) stainless steel pizza pan:** This is the pan to reach for when making the Official Pizza Planet Pie (page 30) as well as all thin crust pizzas. For best crust results, use this with a pizza stone.
- **14-inch (35cm) stainless steel deep dish pizza pan:** Deep dish coming right up! This stainless steel pan has higher sides than your standard pizza pan, allowing you to pile on even more toppings.
- **Half-sheet stainless steel baking pan:** For Sicilian pizza and other rectangular pizzas, this is the only choice.
- **Half-sheet nonstick baking pan:** For some recipes, like calzones and dessert pizza, we prefer the way the nonstick pan cooks.
- **Pizza stone:** How do we get that signature crisp pizza crust? With a pizza stone, of course. Our Pizza Planet Voyagers cook all our pizzas on or near a pizza stone for optimal crusting.
- **Pizza wheel:** How are you going to slice up that pie? Grab a pizza wheel for clean, professional slices. Choose a sturdy one with a comfortable handle.
- **Pizza peel:** Cooking pizza outdoors? Then you need a pizza peel to get that pie on and off the grill or out of the pizza oven. It's also a handy place to slice those thin crust pizzas.
- **Pastry brush:** This essential tool will make quick work of spreading oil on your crust for maximum browning and crispness.

KEY INGREDIENTS

- **Flour:** For most pizza crusts, we use all-purpose flour. This produces a dough that browns nicely even when baked in a home oven. But pizza flour, or 00 flour, is best for outdoor pizza dough because it can withstand the hotter temperatures, browning more slowly.
- **Semolina flour or cornmeal:** We prefer the finer grains of semolina flour for dusting our pizza pans and pizza peels. But yellow cornmeal, which tends to be coarser, can be used as well for good results.
- **Yeast:** Pizza Planet doughs are specifically crafted to be made with the listed yeast. We use active dry yeast in some crusts and rapid-rise yeast in others. Substitute at your own risk!
- **Olive oil:** A key component of Pizza Planet pizzas and other dishes, we recommend a good extra-virgin olive oil to best complement your pizza-making skills.

- **PIZZA PLANET TIP:** You need more toppings than you think you do when making pizzas. Don't shy away from piling it on.

ESSENTIAL CRUSTS *and* SAUCES

Embodying Pizza Planet

Pizza Planet isn't just a restaurant—it's an experience. From the moment guests are cleared for entry through the airlock to the moment they exit the spaceport, they should feel swept into a total star system adventure. That's why it's essential you embody Pizza Planet at all times.

Hungry guests should be directed to the counter to order their space nourishment. Please remember that the White Zone is reserved for passengers who are dining. Those who are looking for more space-themed excitement should be directed to mission control, where they can find a selection of simulators and tools to hone their spaceship-flying skills.

We're thrilled you've suited up to be a Pizza Planet Voyager! Now, get to work . . .

EMPLOYEE OF THE MONTH: THREE ALIENS AWARD

At Pizza Planet, we value the contributions of all our Pizza Planet Voyagers. That's why we recognize one team member each month with the Three Aliens Award.

The award is named for the Three Aliens who stand sentinel as a symbol of protection and enthusiasm at our Pizza Planet registers and in our Pizza Planet trucks. They are the official ambassadors of Pizza Planet.

Look for the Three Aliens Award display in your Pizza Planet break room.

400
200
ML
MADE IN U.S.A.

THIN CRUST PIZZA DOUGH

YIELD: 1 PIZZA CRUST

Pizza Planet's Thin Crust Pizza Dough is our signature dough and used on nearly every thin crust pizza in this book. Pizza Planet caters to a wide array of palates, offering a selection of thin crust dough options for every taste. You'll find that the Whole Wheat Pizza Dough (page 16) and Garlic Basil Pizza Dough (page 57) can both be used interchangeably with this dough.

You do have the option of using a stand mixer to make this dough, but we find the dough tends to be smoother and more elastic when mixed by hand.

For optimal results, we recommend using this dough immediately after making it. But should you want to make it ahead, set the prepared ball in a large oiled bowl and seal with plastic wrap before placing in the fridge instead of rising in a warm place. The dough will need to be brought to room temperature before using. Plan to take it out at least 30 minutes in advance.

INGREDIENTS

⅔ cup (160ml) lukewarm water

1 teaspoon granulated sugar

1½ teaspoons active dry yeast

2 cups (250g) all-purpose flour

1 teaspoon kosher salt

1 tablespoon olive oil, plus 1 tablespoon for greasing the bowl

SPECIAL TOOLS

Stand mixer (optional)

IN A LARGE bowl, combine the lukewarm water and sugar. Stir. Sprinkle the yeast on top and let sit for 3 to 5 minutes until foamy. Add the flour, salt, and olive oil and stir with a rubber spatula until mixed as well as possible. Then, with clean hands, knead the dough, taking care to incorporate smaller bits of dough as you go. Continue until all the dough is one cohesive ball.

POUR THE OLIVE oil into a clean, large bowl and brush to cover the sides. Add the pizza dough and turn to fully coat with oil. Cover with a clean towel and set in a warm place to rise for 1 hour.

Now it's ready to be used to make a pizza.

STAND MIXER INSTRUCTIONS

In a small bowl, combine the water and sugar and stir to combine. Sprinkle with yeast and set aside for 3 to 5 minutes or until foamy. To the bowl of a stand mixer, combine the flour, salt, olive oil, and the yeast mixture. Fitted with the dough hook, run the mixer on low until the ingredients are just incorporated. Increase the speed to medium and let it run for 2 minutes. Stop the mixer and use a rubber spatula to scrape down the sides and turn over the dough, bringing the unmixed portions to the top. Run the mixer for an additional 2 to 3 minutes, or until the dough forms a cohesive ball. Place in the oiled bowl as directed above and allow to rise for an hour before using.

Guest Check

DATE	TABLE	GUESTS	SERVER	ORDER NO.
				102165

ORDER FOR MRS. DAVIS, ANDY'S MOM

Mrs. Davis is Andy and Molly's mom. She's a loving, caring mom who throws fun parties and occasionally makes mistakes, like when she accidentally donates the toys that Andy had intended to store in the attic.

But it's also Andy's mom who gifts Andy his Buzz Lightyear, forever changing the dynamic of Andy's toys. They might even say that is a good thing. Mrs. Davis is also a big fan of Pizza Planet on busy nights.

- The Official Pizza Planet Pie
- Cosmic Loaded Chicken Caesar Bowl
- Stardust Cinnamon Twists

DATE	TABLE	GUESTS	SERVER	ORDER NO.
				102165

WHOLE WHEAT PIZZA DOUGH

YIELD: 1 PIZZA CRUST

Pizza Planet's Whole Wheat Pizza Dough has a nutty, wheat flavor that pairs well with many pizzas in this book, including the Earthling Pizza (page 62). When Pizza Planet patrons are looking for a nutrient-packed option for their pizza crust, this is the go-to.

For optimal results, we recommend using this dough immediately after making it. But same as the Thin Crust Pizza Dough, it can be made ahead. Just set the prepared ball in a large oiled bowl and seal with plastic wrap before placing in the fridge instead of rising in a warm place. The dough will need to be brought to room temperature before using. Plan to take it out at least 30 minutes in advance.

INGREDIENTS

¾ cup (180ml) lukewarm water

1 tablespoon honey

2 teaspoons active dry yeast

2 cups (250g) whole wheat flour

1 tablespoon flaxseed

1 teaspoon kosher salt

2 tablespoons olive oil, plus 1 tablespoon for coating the bowl

IN A LARGE bowl, combine the lukewarm water and honey. Stir. Sprinkle the yeast on top and let sit for 3 to 5 minutes until foamy. Add the whole wheat flour, flaxseed, salt, and olive oil and stir with a rubber spatula until mixed as well as possible. Then, with clean hands, knead the dough, taking care to incorporate smaller bits of dough as you go. Continue until all the dough is one cohesive ball.

POUR THE OLIVE oil into a clean, large bowl and brush to cover the sides. Add the pizza dough and turn to fully coat with oil. Cover with a clean towel and set in a warm place to rise for 1 hour.

Now the dough is ready to be used.

OUTDOOR PIZZA DOUGH

YIELD: 1 BALL PIZZA DOUGH

The high heat of cooking pizza outdoors on a grill or in an outdoor pizza oven requires a slightly different dough without added oil and with a flour better suited to this style of cooking. This will ensure that the pizza can cook without burning. If you cannot find pizza flour, bread flour is your best substitution.

INGREDIENTS

⅔ cup (160ml) lukewarm water

1 teaspoon sugar

1 teaspoon active dry yeast

2 cups (200g) pizza flour (00 flour)

1 teaspoon kosher salt

Cooking oil spray

IN A LARGE bowl, combine the lukewarm water and sugar. Stir. Sprinkle the yeast on top and let sit for 3 to 5 minutes until foamy. Add the flour and salt and stir with a rubber spatula until mixed as well as possible. Then, with clean hands, knead the dough, taking care to incorporate smaller bits of dough as you go. Continue until all the dough is one cohesive ball.

SPRAY A CLEAN, large bowl with cooking oil spray. Add the pizza dough and turn to fully coat with oil. Cover with a clean towel and set in a warm place to rise for 1 hour.

Now it's ready to be used to make a rustic outdoor pizza.

PIZZA PLANET'S SIGNATURE PIZZA SAUCE

YIELD: ABOUT 2 CUPS (500g)

What makes Pizza Planet's pies out of this world? Our signature sauce, of course! This bold sauce filled with herbs, garlic, and a hint of smoky flavor is ready in 5 minutes or less—perfect for getting pizzas to our customers at lightspeed. Use this easy sauce with our signature Thin Crust Pizza Dough (page 14) for a most interstellar experience.

INGREDIENTS

One 14.5-ounce (400g) can fire-roasted diced tomatoes

One 6-ounce (170g) can tomato paste

5 cloves garlic

1 tablespoon dried oregano

1 tablespoon dried basil

1 teaspoon onion powder

1½ teaspoons kosher salt

½ teaspoon ground black pepper

INTO THE BOWL of a food processor, mini food processor, or blender, combine the fire-roasted diced tomatoes (with the juices), tomato paste, garlic, dried oregano, dried basil, onion powder, kosher salt, and ground black pepper. Process until fully combined. Taste and adjust the seasonings as desired.

USE IMMEDIATELY, OR store in the refrigerator in an airtight container until ready to use (up to 1 week).

PIZZA PLANET'S SIGNATURE BARBECUE SAUCE

YIELD: ABOUT 1½ CUPS (420g)

Sweet, tangy, and well-balanced, Pizza Planet's Signature Barbecue Sauce is the base for the Cleared to Enter Barbecue Chicken Pizza (page 44). It also is a popular dip for Woody's Chicken Tenders (page 43). Beware though: The rich, robust flavor is so popular, Pizza Planet customers are always trying to find creative ways to take it home.

INGREDIENTS

One 6-ounce (170g) can tomato paste

½ cup (100g) packed light brown sugar

2 tablespoons apple cider vinegar

2 tablespoons molasses

1 teaspoon kosher salt

1 teaspoon ground mustard

1 teaspoon garlic powder

1 teaspoon onion powder

1 teaspoon paprika

1 teaspoon sriracha hot sauce

½ teaspoon black pepper

IN A SMALL saucepan, whisk together the tomato paste, light brown sugar, apple cider vinegar, molasses, salt, ground mustard, garlic powder, onion powder, paprika, sriracha hot sauce, and black pepper. Cook over medium heat, whisking occasionally, until the mixture begins to bubble in a slow boil. Reduce the heat to medium-low and continue cooking for about 10 minutes, whisking occasionally, until thickened. Remove from the heat. Taste and adjust the seasonings as desired.

TRANSFER TO AN airtight container and chill in the refrigerator for at least 1 hour before using.

THIS SAUCE SHOULD be used within 1 month.

PESTO SAUCE

YIELD: 1 CUP (240g)

For guests seeking an alternative to marinara, pesto is a vibrant way to top a pizza. This sauce can be used in place of marinara on the It's Pizza Classic Cheese Pizza (page 34) and Neptune's Garlic Shrimp Pizza (page 76, but omit the additional garlic).

INGREDIENTS

2 cups (80g) packed basil leaves, washed and dried

1 clove garlic

¼ cup (25g) walnuts

¼ cup (30g) grated Parmesan cheese

½ cup (120ml) olive oil

½ teaspoon kosher salt

IN THE BOWL of a food processor, combine the basil, garlic, walnuts, and Parmesan. Pulse until chopped.

WITH THE FOOD processor running, add the olive oil in a thin stream.

STIR IN THE salt. Taste and add more as desired.

THE PIZZA-MAKING WORKSHOP

How to Work with Pizza Dough

Preparing and Using Dough

Pizza Planet doughs are intended to be used fresh. Ideally, you will make the dough and then cook it into a pizza in the same day, never chilling. But if you want to make the dough in advance, you can. Pizza dough can be made up to 24 hours in advance and stored in an airtight container in the fridge. Remove it from the fridge at least 30 minutes before using, remove the lid of the container and cover with a clean kitchen towel in a warm, dry place. Doing so will give the dough time and space to come to room temperature. Follow the Stretching and Shaping Pizza Dough instructions below.

Stretching and Shaping Pizza Dough

Before you begin working your dough, let it sit at room temperature for 30 to 45 minutes if it has been chilled. A warmer dough will stretch more easily, making it easier to shape. For freshly made dough that was never chilled, it can be used right away.

Next, you'll want to flatten your dough into a round, flat disk with your hands, gently pressing it.

Let it rest for a minute or two before picking up the dough and stretching it with your hands, turning as you go, to achieve a uniform roundness. *(1.1)*

Once you've achieved about the right size and shape, set the dough into your prepared pizza pan. Let it rest for a minute before pressing to expand it fully to the size of the pan and pushing the edges up the pan.

For a thin crust pizza, roll the edges down around the entire pan to form a rim. *(1.2)*

(1.1)

(1.2)

How to Cook Pizza at Home

Want to bring the Pizza Planet experience home? You can with these tips, tricks, and hints for optimal at-home pizza making. But first, check out the tools and ingredients (page 10) section so your kitchen is stocked with everything you need.

Topping Your Pizza

It's always a good idea to gather and measure your ingredients before you start assembling. This will make for an easier and less stressful process.

About Our Two-Bake Method

Cooking pizza at home can be a challenge. To achieve the optimal crust, pizza requires high heat, which can be difficult to achieve in an oven. Fortunately, Pizza Planet has perfected the method, using a combination of a pizza stone and a two-part bake on many of our pizzas.

By placing the pizza tray directly on the pizza stone, the heat hits the crust creating the necessary firmness and doneness to stand up to our most loaded pizzas. The second part of many of the bakes involves finishing the pizza at the top of the oven, where it's farther from the heat source. This allows the crust to brown gently without overcooking the cheese or toppings.

Topping to Perfection

CHEESE BASICS

Customers sometimes are looking for a customized cheese experience. Here's how much to use when they ask for variations.

LIGHT CHEESE: ⅔ cup (80g)

REGULAR CHEESE: 1 cup (115g)

EXTRA CHEESE: 2 cups (230g)

SAUCE BASICS

For those customers who want to customize their sauce experience, here's how much Pizza Planet's Signature Pizza Sauce (page 19) to use:

LIGHT SAUCE: ½ to ⅔ cup (125 to 165g)

REGULAR SAUCE: ¾ to 1 cup (185 to 250g)

EXTRA SAUCE: 1½ to 2 cups (375 to 500g)

Pizza Stone Tip

Pizza stones need to heat up with the oven (ideally for 20 to 30 minutes) to gain and retain heat. Once hot, they transmit that heat.

INTERSTELLAR FAST-FOOD FUELING STATION
Pizza Planet
PIZZA
SALADS
SNACKS
BEVERAGES
SERVING YOUR LOCAL STAR CLUSTER
*GET 1 FREE PIZZA
WHEN YOU ORDER
2 LARGE PIZZAS
MASTER "THE CLAW" IN THE ARCADE

How to Cook Pizza Outdoors

Cooking pizza outdoors on the Pizza Planet grill is a summertime favorite for our customers. But, before you have a table excitedly watching your live pizza-making performance, you need to know a few things.

This technique is intended for a standard gas grill using our Outdoor Pizza Dough recipe (page 19).

Gather Your Toppings

Before getting started, you will need to gather your topping ingredients and measure them so they are ready to be used. Everything you need for the pizza should be with you in the grill area because this method requires rapid cooking.

Prepare Your Dough

Use one ball of Outdoor Pizza Dough (page 19) that's been allowed to rise already. The dough should be at room temperature. If it's been chilled, allow it to sit out for 20 to 30 minutes before using so that it's pliable and easily stretched.

Prepare the surface of a pizza peel by dusting it with flour. Be liberal and ensure the flour extends to the edge of the peel so the dough will transfer easily.

Next, stretch your pizza dough into a thin crust. Outdoor pizzas are more rustic, so it's okay if it ends up more oblong than round. Prick it all over with a fork and brush the top side with olive oil.

Prepare Your Grill

Heat the grill to its highest setting for at least 10 minutes before cooking. You'll also want to grease the grates to ensure the dough doesn't stick.

When it's time to transfer the dough to the grill, gently remove the dough from the pizza peel and set it oil-side down on the grill. Brush the top side with additional olive oil.

Close the grill lid and let it cook for 4 to 6 minutes or until the bottom side has brown grill marks and lightly browned spots. Then use the pizza peel to flip it.

Once flipped, it's time to add your toppings quickly. Spread with sauce, if using, cheese, and other toppings and close the lid. Cook for an additional 4 to 6 minutes and then remove from the grill with the pizza peel.

Although any thin crust pizza recipe can be made outdoors, we recommend these for best results:

- The Official Pizza Planet Pie (page 30)
- It's Pizza Classic Cheese Pizza (page 34)
- Flying Saucer Meatball Pizza (page 38)
- Cleared to Enter Barbecue Chicken Pizza (page 44)
- Strangers from the Outside Buffalo Chicken Pizza (page 41)
- Mercury's Fiery Pizza (page 54, but substitute Outdoor Pizza Dough, page 19)
- The Earthling Pizza (page 62)
- Mars: Red Planet Pie (page 64)

Note: *Do not roll the edges of the pizza dough for outdoor pizza. That step should be omitted from any recipes used.*

Toy Story Trivia

1. Who decorates the plastic utensil that becomes Forky?
2. When Sid grows up, what is his occupation?
3. What color is Andy's cowboy hat?
4. Which of Andy's toys didn't realize he was a toy at first?
5. Who steals Woody from the Davis family tag sale?

ANSWERS: 1. Bonnie, 2. Garbage man, 3. Red, 4. Buzz Lightyear, 5. Al from Al's Toy Barn

Chapter 2
Earthling Favorites
(CLASSIC PIZZAS AND SANDWICHES)

THE OFFICIAL PIZZA PLANET PIE

YIELD: 1 PIZZA (4 SERVINGS)

Ready for the galaxy's best pizza? The Official Pizza Planet Pie is our most popular order for a reason! Inspired by the Pizza Planet logo, our fans love this classic thin crust pizza loaded with our signature sauce along with zesty pepperoni, earthy mushrooms, bright peppers, and onions.

INGREDIENTS

Cooking oil spray

1 teaspoon semolina flour or cornmeal

1 ball Thin Crust Pizza Dough (page 14)

1 tablespoon olive oil

1 cup (250g) Pizza Planet's Signature Pizza Sauce (page 19)

2 cups (8 ounces [225g]) shredded mozzarella cheese

1 green bell pepper, thinly sliced (about ¼ inch [0.5cm] thick)

¾ cup (75g) thinly sliced yellow onion

2 cups (180g) sliced mushrooms

½ cup (140g) pepperoni slices

SPECIAL TOOLS

Pizza stone

16-inch (40cm) round pizza pan

SET ONE OVEN rack at the top of the oven and one at the bottom. On the bottom rack, place a pizza stone. Preheat the oven to 500°F (260°C).

ONCE THE OVEN is heated, begin preparing your pizza. Spray a 16-inch (40cm) round stainless steel pizza pan with cooking oil spray and sprinkle with semolina flour, allowing more to fall toward the center of the pan than the edges.

WITH YOUR HANDS, flatten the pizza dough into a disk. Then let it sit for 1 minute before stretching and turning the dough to form a round, thin crust. Place onto the prepared pizza pan and use your hands to stretch it to the edges and push the dough up the sides of the pan. Once fully stretched, roll the edge of the crust over a little at a time, continuing to work your way around until all the edges have been rolled. Drizzle with the olive oil and use a pastry brush to spread the oil all over, including on the rolled edge of the crust. Prick the dough all over with a fork.

SPREAD THE PIZZA sauce around the pizza into an even layer. Sprinkle with mozzarella cheese evenly and then top with green bell pepper slices, onion slices, sliced mushrooms, and pepperoni.

SLIDE THE PAN into the oven, placing it directly on the pizza stone. Bake for 10 minutes and then transfer the pan to the top rack, baking for an additional 3 to 5 minutes, or until the crust is golden brown.

REMOVE FROM THE oven and let sit for 2 minutes before sliding onto a cutting board or pizza peel and using a pizza wheel to slice into eight slices and serve.

Pizza
Planet
uest Check

VARIATIONS ON A CLASSIC

Pizza Planet Supreme Pizza

Use the following alternative ingredients list, adding the toppings in the order listed. All other instructions should be followed as written.

INGREDIENTS

Cooking oil spray

1 teaspoon semolina flour or cornmeal

1 ball Thin Crust Pizza Dough (page 14)

1 tablespoon olive oil

1 cup (250g) Pizza Planet's Signature Pizza Sauce (page 19)

2 cups (8 ounces [225g]) shredded mozzarella cheese

1 green bell pepper, thinly sliced (about ¼ inch [0.5cm] thick)

¾ cup (75g) thinly sliced yellow onion

2 cups (180g) sliced mushrooms

¼ cup (35g) sliced black olives

½ cup (140g) pepperoni slices

½ pound (225g) crumbled sweet Italian sausage, browned

Pizza Planet Veggie Pizza

Use the following alternative ingredients list, adding the toppings in the order listed. All other instructions should be followed as written.

INGREDIENTS

Cooking oil spray

1 teaspoon semolina flour or cornmeal

1 ball Thin Crust Pizza Dough (page 14)

1 tablespoon olive oil

1 cup (250g) Pizza Planet's Signature Pizza Sauce (page 19)

2 cups (8 ounces [225g]) shredded mozzarella cheese

1 green bell pepper, thinly sliced (about ¼ inch [0.5cm] thick)

¾ cup (75g) thinly sliced yellow onion

2 cups (180g) sliced mushrooms

½ cup (70g) sliced black olives

Pizza Planet Meat Lovers Pizza

Use the following alternative ingredients list, adding the toppings in the order listed. All other instructions should be followed as written.

INGREDIENTS

Cooking oil spray

1 teaspoon semolina flour or cornmeal

1 ball Thin Crust Pizza Dough (page 14)

1 tablespoon olive oil

1 cup (250g) Pizza Planet's Signature Pizza Sauce (page 19)

2 cups (8 ounces [225g]) shredded mozzarella cheese

½ cup (140g) pepperoni slices

½ pound (225g) crumbled sweet Italian sausage, browned

3 Over the Moon Meatballs (page 40), sliced

DATE	TABLE	GUESTS	SERVER	ORDER NO.
				150384

ORDER FOR SID

Sid Phillips is the next-door neighbor of Andy and the Davis family, until they move to a new house. He's well known for his cruel ways with toys—torturing, destroying, and rebuilding them with mismatched parts—and is frequently seen wearing his signature skull shirt. Sid gets lucky while playing the claw game at Pizza Planet and wins both a Buzz Lightyear and Woody after Woody grabs hold of Buzz and won't let go. Woody and Buzz then spend time in Sid's room with all his reconstructed toys, who turn out to be less scary than they look. Sid is pretty mean, until his mismatched toys, together with Woody, come alive in front of him and Woody warns him to "play nice."

- Mercury's Fiery Pizza (to burn my sister's mouth!)
- Orbit Garlic Knots—add Super Nova Sauce
- Galactic Brownies

DATE	TABLE	GUESTS	SERVER	ORDER NO.
				150384

IT'S PIZZA CLASSIC CHEESE PIZZA

YIELD: 1 PIZZA (4 SERVINGS)

A fan favorite! This classic cheese pizza combines our signature sauce with the expected mozzarella cheese and a twist of earthy fresh oregano on a thin crust pizza dough. It's also a signature part of our Voyager training program. Once Pizza Planet Voyagers master this recipe, they can blast off to make any of the Pizza Planet pies!

This pizza can also be made with Whole Wheat Pizza Dough (page 16) or Garlic Basil Pizza Dough (page 57). For those who aren't oregano fans, basil can be substituted.

INGREDIENTS

Cooking oil spray

1 teaspoon semolina flour or cornmeal

1 ball Thin Crust Pizza Dough (page 14)

1 tablespoon olive oil

¾ cup (185g) Pizza Planet's Signature Pizza Sauce (page 19)

2 cups (8 ounces [225g]) shredded mozzarella cheese

1 tablespoon chopped fresh oregano

SET ONE OVEN rack at the top of the oven and one at the bottom. On the bottom rack, place a pizza stone. Preheat the oven to 500°F (260°C).

ONCE THE OVEN is heated, begin preparing your pizza. Spray a 16-inch (40cm) round stainless steel pizza pan with cooking oil spray and sprinkle with semolina flour, allowing more to fall toward the center of the pan than the edges.

WITH YOUR HANDS, flatten the pizza dough into a disk. Then let it sit for 1 minute before stretching and turning the dough to form a round, thin crust. Place onto the prepared pizza pan and use your hands to stretch it to the edges and push the dough up the sides of the pan. Once fully stretched, roll the edge of the crust over a little at a time, continuing to work your way around until all the edges have been rolled. Drizzle with the olive oil and use a pastry brush to spread the oil all over, including on the rolled edge of the crust. Prick the dough all over with a fork.

SPREAD THE PIZZA sauce around the pizza into an even layer. Sprinkle with mozzarella cheese evenly and then top with oregano.

SLIDE THE PAN into the oven, placing it directly on the pizza stone. Bake for 10 minutes and then transfer the pan to the top rack, baking for an additional 2 to 3 minutes, or until the crust is golden brown.

REMOVE FROM THE oven and let sit for 2 minutes before sliding onto a cutting board or pizza peel and using a pizza wheel to slice into eight slices and serve.

Pizza Planet
CAUTION: HOT PIZZA
SERVING YOUR LOCAL STAR CLUSTER
Pizza Planet

GREEN ALIEN PIE

YIELD: 1 PIZZA (4 SERVINGS)

The claaaaaaaaaaaaaw! If this pie could talk, that's what it would be saying as our fans reach for slice after slice. Loaded with earthy spinach, zesty red onions, sweet cherry tomatoes, and bright herbs, this pizza is a hit with vegetable pizza lovers. For the pizza dough, either the Thin Crust Pizza Dough (page 14) or Whole Wheat Pizza Dough (page 16) will do the trick.

INGREDIENTS

Cooking oil spray

1 teaspoon semolina flour or cornmeal

1 ball pizza dough

1 tablespoon olive oil

1 cup (250g) Pizza Planet's Signature Pizza Sauce (page 19)

2 cups (8 ounces [225g]) shredded mozzarella cheese

4 cups (120g) baby spinach

1 cup (100g) quartered and thinly sliced red onions

1 cup (170g) cherry tomatoes, halved

2 tablespoons chopped fresh oregano

¼ cup (15g) sliced fresh basil

SET ONE OVEN rack at the top of the oven and one at the bottom. On the bottom rack, place a pizza stone. Preheat the oven to 500°F (260°C).

ONCE THE OVEN is heated, begin preparing your pizza. Spray a 16-inch (40cm) round stainless steel pizza pan with cooking oil spray and sprinkle with semolina flour, allowing more to fall toward the center of the pan than the edges.

WITH YOUR HANDS, flatten the pizza dough into a disk. Then let it sit for 1 minute before stretching and turning the dough to form a round, thin crust. Place onto the prepared pizza pan and use your hands to stretch it to the edges and push the dough up the sides of the pan. Once fully stretched, roll the edge of the crust over a little at a time, continuing to work your way around until all the edges have been rolled. Drizzle with the olive oil and use a pastry brush to spread the oil all over, including on the rolled edge of the crust. Prick the dough all over with a fork.

SPREAD THE PIZZA sauce around the pizza into an even layer. Sprinkle with mozzarella cheese evenly and then top with baby spinach, red onions, cherry tomatoes, oregano, and basil.

SLIDE THE PAN into the oven, placing it directly on the pizza stone. Bake for 10 minutes and then transfer the pan to the top rack, baking for an additional 4 to 5 minutes, or until the crust is golden brown.

REMOVE FROM THE oven and let sit for 2 minutes before sliding onto a cutting board or pizza peel and using a pizza wheel to slice into eight slices and serve.

FLYING SAUCER MEATBALL PIZZA

YIELD: 1 PIZZA (4 SERVINGS)

Landing on a Pizza Planet near you, the Flying Saucer Meatball Pizza is a bold, meaty pie that will transport you to the cosmos. Big slices of our signature Over the Moon Meatballs and our distinctive Pizza Planet's Signature Pizza Sauce make this pizza unforgettable. If you don't have grated Romano cheese, Parmesan can be substituted.

INGREDIENTS

Cooking oil spray

1 teaspoon semolina flour or cornmeal

1 ball Thin Crust Pizza Dough (page 14)

1 tablespoon olive oil

¾ cup (180g) Pizza Planet's Signature Pizza Sauce (page 19)

2 cups (8 ounces [225g]) shredded mozzarella cheese

3 Over the Moon Meatballs (page 40), sliced

1 tablespoon fresh chopped basil

1 tablespoon grated Romano cheese

SET ONE OVEN rack at the top of the oven and one at the bottom. On the bottom rack, place a pizza stone. Preheat the oven to 525°F (275°C).

ONCE THE OVEN is heated, begin preparing your pizza. Spray a 16-inch (40cm) round stainless steel pizza pan with cooking oil spray and sprinkle with semolina flour, allowing more to fall toward the center of the pan than the edges.

WITH YOUR HANDS, flatten the pizza dough into a disk. Then let it sit for 1 minute before stretching and turning the dough to form a round, thin crust. Place onto the prepared pizza pan and use your hands to stretch it to the edges and push the dough up the sides of the pan. Once fully stretched, roll the edge of the crust over a little at a time, continuing to work your way around until all the edges have been rolled. Drizzle with the olive oil and use a pastry brush to spread the oil all over, including on the rolled edge of the crust. Prick the dough all over with a fork.

SPREAD THE PIZZA sauce around the pizza into an even layer. Sprinkle with mozzarella cheese evenly and then top with sliced meatballs, fresh chopped basil, and Romano cheese.

SLIDE THE PAN into the oven, placing it directly on the pizza stone. Bake for 10 minutes and then transfer the pan to the top rack, baking for an additional 5 to 7 minutes, or until the crust is golden brown.

REMOVE FROM THE oven and let sit for 2 minutes before sliding onto a cutting board or pizza peel and using a pizza wheel to slice into eight slices and serve.

Over the Moon Meatballs

YIELD: 6 LARGE MEATBALLS (6 SERVINGS, AS AN APPETIZER)

They're so big, they're massive! These tender, flavorful meatballs are excellent on our Flying Saucer Meatball Pizza (page 38). They also make an excellent appetizer on their own. Or use them in our Protoplanet Meatball Parm Grinder (page 47) with marinara and mozzarella for a galactic sandwich.

INGREDIENTS

Cooking oil spray

1 cup (40g) fresh breadcrumbs (from sandwich bread)

2 tablespoons milk

1 pound (450g) ground beef

4 cups (460g) grated Parmesan cheese

1 large egg, beaten

2 teaspoons dried basil

1 teaspoon dried oregano

1 teaspoon garlic powder

1 teaspoon onion powder

1 teaspoon kosher salt

½ teaspoon pepper

PREHEAT THE OVEN to 400°F (200°C). Spray a 9-by-13-inch (23-by-33cm) rectangular glass baking pan with cooking oil spray and set aside.

IN A LARGE mixing bowl, mix together the breadcrumbs and milk. Add the ground beef, Parmesan, egg, dried basil, dried oregano, garlic powder, onion powder, salt, and pepper and stir and knead until fully incorporated. Working with a small part of the meat mixture at a time, roll into six meatballs (roughly 3 inches [7.5cm] in diameter) and place in the baking pan, not touching.

SLIDE INTO THE oven and bake for 20 to 25 minutes, until cooked through. Serve them up in the Flying Saucer Meatball Pizza or try them with pasta or in a sub!

OVER THE MOON Meatballs can also be topped with Pizza Planet's Signature Pizza Sauce (page 19)—about 1 tablespoon, warmed, per meatball—and a sprinkle of Parmesan or Romano cheese for a delightful appetizer variation.

STRANGERS FROM THE OUTSIDE BUFFALO CHICKEN PIZZA

YIELD: 1 PIZZA (4 SERVINGS)

Our little green alien friends guard Pizza Planet delivery trucks all over. And when they see unexpected visitors climb inside, they call them Strangers from the Outside. Likewise, this bold and spicy signature pizza is like a stranger next to Pizza Planet's more classic fare, but it's welcome all the same. Piled with spicy buffalo sauce, creamy mozzarella cheese, crisp breaded chicken and bacon, and pungent red onions, this pie is finished with a bold sprinkle of crumbled blue cheese.

INGREDIENTS

Cooking oil spray

1 teaspoon semolina flour or cornmeal

1 ball Thin Crust Pizza Dough (page 14)

1 tablespoon olive oil

⅓ cup (90g) buffalo sauce

2 cups (8 ounces [225g]) shredded mozzarella cheese

½ pound (225g) Woody's Chicken Tenders (page 43), sliced

3 slices thick-cut bacon, lightly browned and chopped

½ cup (50g) thinly sliced red onions (⅛ inch [3mm] thick)

¼ cup (35g) crumbled blue cheese

SET ONE OVEN rack at the top of the oven and one at the bottom. On the bottom rack, place a pizza stone. Preheat the oven to 500°F (260°C).

ONCE THE OVEN is heated, begin preparing your pizza. Spray a 16-inch (40cm) round stainless steel pizza pan with cooking oil spray and sprinkle with semolina flour, allowing more to fall toward the center of the pan than the edges.

WITH YOUR HANDS, flatten the pizza dough into a disk. Then let it sit for 1 minute before stretching and turning the dough to form a round, thin crust. Place onto the prepared pizza pan and use your hands to stretch it to the edges and push the dough up the sides of the pan. Once fully stretched, roll the edge of the crust over a little at a time, continuing to work your way around until all the edges have been rolled. Drizzle with the olive oil and use a pastry brush to spread the oil all over, including on the rolled edge of the crust. Prick the dough all over with a fork.

SLIDE THE PIZZA crust into the oven, placing the pan directly on the pizza stone. Bake for 10 minutes.

REMOVE FROM THE oven and spread buffalo sauce over the pizza dough. Top with mozzarella cheese, spreading evenly over the surface. Sprinkle with sliced chicken tenders, chopped bacon, and sliced red onions.

SLIDE THE PIZZA pan into the oven on the top rack and bake for 5 to 7 minutes, turning once, or until the crust is lightly browned all over. Remove from the oven and sprinkle with blue cheese.

LET SIT FOR 2 minutes before sliding onto a cutting board or pizza peel and using a pizza wheel to slice into eight slices and serve.

Woody's Chicken Tenders

YIELD: 4 SERVINGS (ABOUT 2 TENDERS PER SERVING)

A key component of our Strangers from the Outside Buffalo Chicken Pizza (page 41), these crispy chicken tenders are also delightful on their own. They are often ordered as an appetizer as well. Choices of dipping sauce include buffalo sauce, barbecue sauce, and Super Nova Sauce (page 49). These are named for the classic toy, Woody, from Woody's Roundup. Rumor has it that one lucky Pizza Planet fan once won a Woody toy in the claw machine game!

INGREDIENTS

1 cup (115g) all-purpose flour

1 teaspoon kosher salt

1 teaspoon black pepper

2 large eggs, beaten

1 cup (100g) panko breadcrumbs

2 tablespoons canola oil

1 pound (450g) raw chicken tenders

IN A SHALLOW bowl, sift together the flour, salt, and pepper. Put the eggs in a second shallow bowl. Put the panko breadcrumbs in a third shallow bowl. Line up near the stove for easy dredging.

IN A LARGE skillet, heat the canola oil over medium heat. Once it's hot, dredge the chicken tenders one at a time, first in the flour mixture, then in the egg mixture, and finally in the panko mixture, taking care to thoroughly coat them. Place into the pan with the hot oil.

COOK FOR 4 to 5 minutes per side until golden brown all over. Remove the chicken tenders from the pan as they complete cooling, setting them on a plate. Once all the tenders have been cooked, they are ready to be eaten or used in other recipes.

CHARACTER CALLOUT: WOODY

Sheriff Woody Pride is the rootinest tootinest cowboy who tells his fans, "You're my favorite deputy!" He's a pretty special cowboy, with a hand-painted face, natural-dyed, blanket-stitched vest, and a hand-stretched polyvinyl hat. A natural leader, Woody also has a jealous side and can occasionally get annoyed with the other toys, like when Buzz Lightyear becomes one of Andy's toys. Woody worries he's being replaced but also makes sure Buzz isn't alone when Sid captures him with the claw and takes him home. But Woody and Buzz eventually find common ground and become an unlikely pair of friends.

CLEARED TO ENTER BARBECUE CHICKEN PIZZA

YIELD: 1 PIZZA (4 SERVINGS)

When visitors arrive at Pizza Planet, our planet safety system clears them to enter. It's a key part of the Pizza Planet experience. And once inside, our fans have come to expect big, bold pizza pies like this Barbecue Chicken Pizza. Loaded with rich barbecue sauce, this pie has meaty grilled chicken and sweet bell pepper. But don't reach for the mozzarella. To make this pie perfect, you'll need cheddar cheese.

INGREDIENTS

Cooking oil spray

1 teaspoon semolina flour or cornmeal

1 ball pizza dough

¾ cup (210g) Pizza Planet's Signature Barbecue Sauce (page 20)

2 cups (230g) grated cheddar cheese

1 cup (170g) diced grilled chicken

1 sweet bell pepper, thinly sliced

SET ONE OVEN rack at the top of the oven and one at the bottom. On the bottom rack, place a pizza stone. Preheat the oven to 525°F (275°C).

ONCE THE OVEN is heated, begin preparing your pizza. Spray a 16-inch (40cm) round stainless steel pizza pan with cooking oil spray and sprinkle with semolina flour, allowing more to fall toward the center of the pan than the edges.

WITH YOUR HANDS, flatten the pizza dough into a disk. Then let it sit for 1 minute before stretching and turning the dough to form a round, thin crust. Place onto the prepared pizza pan and use your hands to stretch it to the edges and push the dough up the sides of the pan. Once fully stretched, roll the edge of the crust over a little at a time, continuing to work your way around until all the edges have been rolled. Prick the dough all over with a fork.

SPREAD THE BARBECUE sauce around the pizza into an even layer. Sprinkle with cheddar cheese evenly and then top with diced chicken and sliced peppers.

SLIDE THE PAN into the oven, placing it directly on the pizza stone. Bake for 10 minutes and then transfer the pan to the top rack, baking for an additional 5 to 7 minutes, or until the crust is golden brown.

REMOVE FROM THE oven and let sit for 2 minutes before sliding onto a cutting board or pizza peel and using a pizza wheel to slice into eight slices and serve.

PROTOPLANET CHICKEN PARM GRINDER (PICTURED)

YIELD: 4 SANDWICHES (4 SERVINGS)

Pizza Planet isn't sleeping on pizza parlor classics! This Chicken Parm Grinder features freshly fried chicken breasts on warm rolls with marinara and mozzarella. We don't call this one a classic for nothing!

INGREDIENTS

1 cup (115g) all-purpose flour

1 teaspoon kosher salt

1 teaspoon black pepper

1 teaspoon oregano

1 teaspoon paprika

2 eggs, beaten

1 cup (100g) panko breadcrumbs

2 tablespoons olive oil

1 pound (450g) chicken breast, pounded to ½-inch (1.5cm) thickness and cut into 4 oblong pieces

4 hoagie rolls, sliced open

¾ cup (190g) marinara sauce

¾ cup (90g) grated mozzarella cheese

PREHEAT THE OVEN to 375°F (190°C).

IN A SHALLOW bowl, sift together the flour, salt, pepper, oregano, and paprika. Put the beaten eggs in a second shallow bowl. Put the panko breadcrumbs in a third shallow bowl.

IN A LARGE skillet, heat 1 tablespoon of oil over medium heat and swirl around the pan. Once it's hot, dredge the chicken pieces, one at a time, in the flour mixture, then the egg, and then the panko. Place in the skillet and fry until golden brown on both sides and cooked through (about 4 to 6 minutes per side) turning once. Remove from the heat.

PUT EACH OF the four rolls on a separate square of aluminum foil. Add a chicken breast to each. Spoon marinara sauce into each roll and top with the mozzarella. Close the aluminum foil around the sandwich, leaving the top exposed, and add more mozzarella.

BAKE FOR 5 to 8 minutes, or until the mozzarella is melted.

CUT IN HALF and serve.

Protoplanet Meatball Parm Grinder (NOT PICTURED)

YIELD: 4 SANDWICHES (4 SERVINGS)

This variation of the Protoplanet Chicken Parm Grinder is another pizza parlor classic. Hoagie rolls are topped with our well-seasoned, meaty meatballs along with marinara sauce and mozzarella for an interstellar cheesy, meaty experience.

INGREDIENTS

4 hoagie rolls, sliced open

1 batch Over the Moon Meatballs (page 40)

¾ cup (190g) marinara sauce

¾ cup (90g) grated mozzarella cheese

PREHEAT THE OVEN to 375°F (190°C).

PUT EACH OF the four rolls on a separate square of aluminum foil. Cut the meatballs in half and place three halves on each roll. Spoon marinara sauce onto and around the meatballs and top with the mozzarella. Close the aluminum foil around the sandwich, leaving the top exposed and add more mozzarella.

BAKE FOR 5 to 8 minutes, or until the mozzarella is melted.

CUT IN HALF and serve.

SUPER NOVA BURGER

YIELD: 4 BURGERS (4 SERVINGS)

Pizza Planet is more than pizza! The Super Nova Burger is our signature sandwich, featuring a seasoned beef patty topped with fresh lettuce, juicy tomato, sharp cheddar, smoky bacon, and our complex Super Nova Sauce. When your customer isn't feeling pizza, suggest this spectacular option.

INGREDIENTS

1 pound (450g) ground beef

½ teaspoon kosher salt

¼ teaspoon black pepper

4 slices sharp cheddar cheese

4 brioche hamburger buns

4 leaves romaine lettuce

12 slices bacon, browned

4 slices tomato

Super Nova Sauce (recipe below)

DIVIDE THE GROUND beef into four equal portions and shape each into a round patty about ½ inch thick and 5 inches wide (1.5cm thick and 13cm wide). Sprinkle all over with salt and pepper.

PREHEAT THE GRILL to medium heat and cook the burgers, flipping once, to the desired doneness. For medium, cook for 3 to 4 minutes per side.

PLACE A SLICE of cheddar on each burger and allow to soften for 30 seconds before removing the burgers from the grill.

IF DESIRED, TOAST the buns on the grill as well.

NOW IT'S TIME to prepare the burgers for serving.

PLACE ONE ROLL on each of four plates and top with the lettuce, broken down to fit the roll, followed by the burger, bacon, tomato, and sauce. Serve immediately.

Super Nova Sauce

YIELD: ABOUT ⅔ CUP (160ml)

Creamy, zesty, fresh, and fun, this Super Nova Sauce is the key component of our Super Nova Burger (recipe above). It's also a lovely complement for Woody's Chicken Tenders (page 43).

INGREDIENTS

¼ cup (60ml) mayonnaise

¼ cup (35g) finely chopped yellow onion

1 tablespoon plus 1 teaspoon ketchup

1 tablespoon relish

1 teaspoon Dijon mustard

1 teaspoon chili garlic sauce

IN A SMALL mixing bowl, whisk together the mayonnaise, onion, ketchup, relish, mustard, and chili garlic sauce until smooth. Use this sauce on burgers or sandwiches . . . or recommend it to a guest for their fries.

FIERY BIG BANG CHICKEN SANDWICH

YIELD: 4 SANDWICHES (4 SERVINGS)

For customers who love a sandwich that brings the heat, the Fiery Big Bang Chicken Sandwich delivers. In this recipe, you'll top a traditional hamburger bun with a freshly fried and buffalo sauce–glazed chicken patty, sharp cheddar, zesty red onions, crisp lettuce, and funky blue cheese. For diners who like it extra hot, we recommend serving with a side of additional buffalo sauce for dipping. This is also excellent served as a salad. Omit the roll and romaine lettuce and instead serve on a bed (1 cup [50g]) of shredded iceberg lettuce.

INGREDIENTS

1 pound (450g) boneless, skinless chicken breasts

2 large eggs

⅔ cup (80g) all-purpose flour

1 teaspoon salt

½ teaspoon pepper

⅔ cup (65g) Italian breadcrumbs

1 tablespoon olive oil

½ cup (140g) buffalo sauce

4 slices sharp cheddar cheese

4 hamburger buns

4 leaves romaine lettuce

4 slices (⅛ inch [3mm] thick) red onion

4 ounces (115g) blue cheese, crumbled

USE A MEAT mallet to pound the chicken to about ¼ inch (0.5cm) thick. Cut into four pieces (one per sandwich).

WHISK THE EGGS in a shallow bowl. In another shallow bowl, stir together the flour, salt, and pepper. Put the breadcrumbs in a third shallow bowl.

IN A LARGE skillet, heat the oil. Once hot, dredge each chicken piece in the flour mixture, then the egg mixture, and then in the breadcrumbs before adding to the hot oil. Continue until all the chicken is in the pan.

COOK, FLIPPING ONCE, until golden brown and cooked through, 4 to 6 minutes per side. Pour the buffalo sauce over the chicken and top each with a slice of cheddar. Cover the pan and cook for an additional 2 minutes to allow the sauce to absorb.

TRANSFER ONE CHICKEN breast patty to each of the hamburger buns. Top with a romaine leaf, tearing into smaller pieces to fit, and a red onion slice. Finish with the blue cheese and serve.

Chapter 3

Out-of-This-World SPECIALTY PIZZAS

MERCURY'S FIERY PIZZA

YIELD: 1 PIZZA (4 SERVINGS)

Like the closest planet to the sun, this pizza is hot. But it's also nuanced with sweet pineapple, rich ham, and zesty red onion on our herby Garlic Basil Pizza Dough (page 57). Finished with a drizzle of hot honey, this is a pie for grown-ups and the bravest of pizza lovers.

INGREDIENTS

Cooking oil spray

1 teaspoon semolina flour or cornmeal

1 ball Garlic Basil Pizza Dough (page 57)

1 tablespoon olive oil

⅔ cup (165g) Pizza Planet's Signature Pizza Sauce (page 19)

2 cups (230g) shredded mozzarella cheese

1 cup (150g) diced ham

One 8-ounce (225g) can pineapple chunks, drained

½ cup (70g) diced red onions

1 teaspoon hot honey

SET ONE OVEN rack at the top of the oven and one at the bottom. On the bottom rack, place a pizza stone. Preheat the oven to 525°F (275°C).

ONCE THE OVEN is heated, begin preparing your pizza. Spray a 16-inch (40cm) round stainless steel pizza pan with cooking oil spray and sprinkle with semolina flour, allowing more to fall toward the center of the pan than the edges.

WITH YOUR HANDS, flatten the pizza dough into a disk. Then let it sit for 1 minute before stretching and turning the dough to form a round, thin crust. Place onto the prepared pizza pan and use your hands to stretch it to the edges and push the dough up the sides of the pan. Once fully stretched, roll the edge of the crust over a little at a time, continuing to work your way around until all the edges have been rolled. Drizzle with the olive oil and use a pastry brush to spread the oil all over, including on the rolled edge of the crust. Prick the dough all over with a fork.

SPREAD PIZZA SAUCE evenly around the crust and top with mozzarella cheese. Sprinkle with ham, pineapple chunks, and diced red onions.

SLIDE THE PAN into the oven, placing it directly on the pizza stone. Bake for 10 minutes and then transfer the pan to the top rack, baking for an additional 5 to 6 minutes, or until the crust is golden brown.

REMOVE FROM THE oven and drizzle with hot honey. Let sit for 2 minutes before sliding onto a cutting board or pizza peel and using a pizza wheel to slice into eight slices and serve.

Mercury Trivia

1. What is the closest planet to the sun in our galaxy?
2. How hot does the surface of Mercury get?
3. How long is a year on Mercury?
4. Mercury is named after the ____ Roman god.
5. Mercury does not have an ____ to regulate surface temperature.

ANSWERS: . Mercury, 2. 800 degrees Fahrenheit (425 degrees Celsius), 3. 88 days, 4. fastest, 5. atmosphere

Garlic Basil Pizza Dough

YIELD: 1 PIZZA CRUST

Pizza Planet's Thin Crust Pizza Dough gets an herby twist in this garlic-basil remix.

INGREDIENTS

⅔ cup (160ml) lukewarm water

1 teaspoon granulated sugar

1½ teaspoons active dry yeast

2 cups (250g) all-purpose flour

1 teaspoon kosher salt

1 teaspoon dried basil

1 teaspoon garlic powder

1 tablespoon olive oil, plus 1 tablespoon for greasing the bowl

IN A LARGE bowl, combine the lukewarm water and sugar. Stir. Sprinkle the yeast on top and let sit for 3 to 5 minutes until foamy. Add the flour, salt, basil, garlic powder, and olive oil and stir with a rubber spatula until mixed as well as possible. Then, with clean hands, knead the dough, taking care to incorporate smaller bits of dough as you go. Continue until all the dough is one cohesive ball.

POUR THE OLIVE oil into a clean, large bowl and brush to cover the sides. Add the pizza dough and turn to fully coat with oil. Cover with a clean towel and place in a warm place to rise for 1 hour before using to make a pizza.

Pizza Planet
PIZZA
STAR CLUSTER

THE VENUS-STYLE (INSIDE-OUT) PIZZA

YIELD: 1 PIZZA (4 SERVINGS)

Venus, the second planet from the Sun, is close in size to Earth but largely considered to be its opposite with high heat on the surface and a dense atmosphere. That denseness and heat is captured in the Venus-Style (Inside-Out) Pizza, a Chicago deep dish pizza with layers of cheese, sausage, onion, pepper, and tomato on top. This hearty, loaded pizza with a robust crust and loads of cheese is a menu favorite among Pizza Planet fans.

INGREDIENTS

1 Deep Dish Pizza Dough (page 60)

4 cups (1 pound [450g]) shredded mozzarella cheese

1 pound (450g) sweet Italian ground sausage, browned

2 cups (500g) Pizza Planet's Signature Pizza Sauce (page 19)

1 green bell pepper, thinly sliced

1 cup (100g) thinly sliced yellow onion

½ cup (60g) grated Romano or Parmesan cheese

1 teaspoon dried oregano

SPECIAL TOOLS

14-inch (35cm) stainless steel deep dish pizza pan

Pizza stone

PREHEAT THE OVEN to 475°F (245°C). Make sure one oven rack is place on the lowest setting with a pizza stone on it and the other placed close to the top.

MEANWHILE, IN A 14-inch (35cm) stainless steel deep dish pizza pan, spread the dough to cover the bottom and creep up the sides to the top. Prick all over with a fork. Cover with a towel and let rise in a warm place for 20 minutes.

SLIDE THE PIZZA pan into the oven, onto the pizza stone, and bake for 5 minutes. Remove from the oven. Spread the cheese evenly over the crust. Top with the browned Italian sausage. Drizzle the pizza sauce all over, spreading it evenly. Top with the green bell pepper and onion and then sprinkle with Romano cheese and oregano.

SLIDE INTO THE oven onto the pizza stone and bake for 25 minutes. Move the pan to the top rack and cook for an additional 5 to 7 minutes or until the crust is golden brown.

REMOVE FROM THE oven and let sit for 5 minutes before cutting into eight slices and serving.

Deep Dish Pizza Dough

YIELD: 1 BALL OF PIZZA DOUGH, ENOUGH FOR ONE 14-INCH (35CM) DEEP DISH PIZZA

Deep dish pizza needs a firm, strong dough to stand up to the heavy load of toppings. Laced with cornmeal, this crust has a distinctive texture that's both soft on the inside and a bit flaky on the outside. Delightful!

INGREDIENTS

1 envelope (7g) rapid-rise dry yeast

2¾ cups (340g) all-purpose flour

⅓ cup (45g) cornmeal

1 teaspoon salt

1 teaspoon sugar

2 tablespoons olive oil, plus more for greasing the bowl

1 cup (240ml) lukewarm water

SPECIAL TOOLS

Stand mixer

IN THE BOWL of a stand mixer, sift together the yeast, flour, cornmeal, salt, and sugar. Add the olive oil and lukewarm water. Fitted with the dough hook, turn the mixer on low and mix until a dough begins to form. Turn the mixer to medium speed and mix for 2 minutes. Stop the mixer, scrape down the sides, and turn the dough over, bringing the unmixed bits to the top. Turn the mixer on medium and mix for an additional 3 to 5 minutes, or until a cohesive ball forms.

RUB A LARGE bowl with oil and add the dough, turning to coat. Cover with a towel and let rise in a warm place for 1 hour.

USE IN RECIPES that call for deep dish pizza dough.

DATE	TABLE	GUESTS	SERVER	ORDER NO.
				120661

ORDER FOR AL

Al McWhiggin is the owner of Al's Toy Barn, but to Andy's toys, he's the Chicken Man. After all, he dons a chicken costume for a TV ad. This collector of all things Woody's Roundup is greedy, impulsive, and impatient. He even steals Woody from the Davis family tag sale. Al has been collecting the toys from Woody's Roundup when he steals Woody, has him repaired, and prepares to sell the whole collection to a museum in Japan. Fortunately, he's thwarted, and Woody returns to Andy's room with Bullseye and Jessie. Pizza Planet Voyagers, be warned, you want to deliver fast to this customer. He's a big fan of our delivery service.

- Super Nova Burger
- Double Super Nova Sauce
- ~~2~~ 3 Pizza Planet Mega Gulp Frozen Strawberry Lemonades
- Side: Pickles. No, wait. Extra pickles.

DATE	TABLE	GUESTS	SERVER	ORDER NO.
				120661

THE EARTHLING PIZZA

YIELD: 1 PIZZA (4 SERVINGS)

Much like the pizza named for Earth's sister planet, Venus, this pizza is piled with sausage, onion, and pepper. But just like the planetary pair, the Earthling Pizza is the opposite of the Venus with a thin wheat crust and toppings layered on lighter, in the thin crust style.

INGREDIENTS

Cooking oil spray

1 teaspoon semolina flour or cornmeal

1 ball Whole Wheat Pizza Dough (page 16)

1 tablespoon olive oil

1 cup (250g) Pizza Planet's Signature Pizza Sauce (page 19)

2 cups (8 ounces [225g]) mozzarella cheese

½ pound (225g) crumbled sweet Italian sausage, browned

1 cup (100g) thinly sliced onion

1 green bell pepper, seeded and thinly sliced

SET ONE OVEN rack at the top of the oven and one at the bottom. On the bottom rack, place a pizza stone. Preheat the oven to 525°F (275°C).

ONCE THE OVEN is heated, begin preparing your pizza. Spray a 16-inch (40cm) round stainless steel pizza pan with cooking oil spray and sprinkle with semolina flour, allowing more to fall toward the center of the pan than the edges.

WITH YOUR HANDS, flatten the pizza dough into a disk. Then let it sit for 1 minute before stretching and turning the dough to form a round, thin crust. Place onto the prepared pizza pan and use your hands to stretch it to the edges and push the dough up the sides of the pan. Once fully stretched, roll the edge of the crust over a little at a time, continuing to work your way around until all the edges have been rolled. Drizzle with the olive oil and use a pastry brush to spread the oil all over, including on the rolled edge of the crust. Prick the dough all over with a fork.

SPREAD PIZZA SAUCE evenly around the crust and top with mozzarella cheese. Sprinkle all over with sausage, onion, and bell pepper.

SLIDE THE PAN into the oven, placing it directly on the pizza stone. Bake for 10 minutes and then transfer the pan to the top rack, baking for an additional 5 to 6 minutes, or until the crust is golden brown.

REMOVE FROM THE oven and let sit for 2 minutes before sliding onto a cutting board or pizza peel and using a pizza wheel to slice into eight slices and serve.

MARS: RED PLANET PIE

YIELD: 1 PIZZA (4 SERVINGS)

Much like the Red Planet itself, this is no ordinary pie! What secrets does this popular pie hold? Piled with bright tomato, zesty garlic, and bright basil, this one has two cheeses and no sauce—and it's incredible. Suggest it to adventurous guests who want something a little different.

INGREDIENTS

Cooking oil spray

1 teaspoon semolina flour or cornmeal

1 ball pizza dough, such as Thin Crust Pizza Dough (page 14) or Garlic Basil Pizza Dough (page 57)

1 tablespoon olive oil

1 cup (4 ounces [115g]) shredded mozzarella cheese

1 large tomato, sliced

2 cloves garlic, minced

¼ cup (15g) fresh basil leaves plus ¼ cup (15g) thinly sliced fresh basil leaves, divided

½ cup (60g) grated Parmesan or Romano cheese

SET ONE OVEN rack at the top of the oven and one at the bottom. On the bottom rack, place a pizza stone. Preheat the oven to 500°F (260°C).

ONCE THE OVEN is heated, begin preparing your pizza. Spray a 16-inch (40cm) round stainless steel pizza pan with cooking oil spray and sprinkle with semolina flour, allowing more to fall toward the center of the pan than the edges.

WITH YOUR HANDS, flatten the pizza dough into a disk. Then let it sit for 1 minute before stretching and turning the dough to form a round, thin crust. Place onto the prepared pizza pan and use your hands to stretch it to the edges and push the dough up the sides of the pan. Once fully stretched, roll the edge of the crust over a little at a time, continuing to work your way around until all the edges have been rolled. Drizzle with the olive oil and use a pastry brush to spread the oil all over, including on the rolled edge of the crust. Prick the dough all over with a fork.

SPREAD MOZZARELLA CHEESE evenly around the crust and top with tomato slices. Sprinkle with minced garlic, ¼ cup (15g) of fresh basil leaves, and Parmesan cheese.

SLIDE THE PAN into the oven, placing it directly on the pizza stone. Bake for 10 minutes and then transfer the pan to the top rack, baking for an additional 5 to 6 minutes, or until the crust is golden brown.

REMOVE FROM THE oven and top with the remaining ¼ cup (15g) of thinly sliced fresh basil leaves. Let sit for 2 minutes before sliding onto a cutting board or pizza peel and using a pizza wheel to slice into eight slices and serve.

Mars Trivia

1. Which planet in our solar system is nicknamed the Red Planet?
2. What are the names of Mars's moons?
3. Mars has the tallest _____ in our solar system.
4. Mars is named after the Roman god of _____.
5. What is the average temperature on Mars?

ANSWERS: 1. Mars, 2. Phobos and Deimos, 3. volcano, 4. war, 5. -85 degrees Fahrenheit (-65 degrees Celsius)

JUPITER PIE (IT'S MASSIVE!)

YIELD: 1 PIZZA (4 SERVINGS)

There's no way around it: This pizza is a giant among giants. Two kinds of meat and three veggies! If a guest is struggling to picture it, you can tell them this massive rectangle pizza is a thin crust with a twist. Think school pizza for grown-ups!

INGREDIENTS

Cooking oil spray

1 teaspoon semolina flour or cornmeal

1 ball Thin Crust Pizza Dough (page 14)

1 cup (250g) Pizza Planet's Signature Pizza Sauce (page 19)

2 cups (8 ounces [225g]) shredded mozzarella cheese

½ pound (3 links [225g]) sweet Italian sausage, cooked and sliced

½ cup (140g) pepperoni slices

2 cups (120g) broccoli florets

1 cup (140g) sweet bell pepper, sliced

One 8-ounce (225g) can sliced black olives, drained

PREHEAT THE OVEN to 500°F (260°C). Set the pizza rack in the middle of the oven.

ONCE THE OVEN is heated, begin preparing your pizza. Line a 9-by-13-inch (23-by-33cm) nonstick baking tray with parchment paper. Spray with cooking oil spray and sprinkle with semolina flour, allowing more to fall toward the center of the pan than the edges.

WITH YOUR HANDS, flatten the pizza dough into a rectangle. Then let it sit for 1 minute before stretching and turning the dough to form a larger rectangle crust. Place onto the prepared pan and use your hands to stretch it to the edges. Let it rest for a few minutes if it resists before continuing. Prick the dough all over with a fork.

SPREAD PIZZA SAUCE evenly over the crust and top with mozzarella cheese, spreading to the edges of the pizza. Top with sliced sausage, pepperoni, broccoli, bell pepper slices, and olive slices.

SLIDE THE PAN into the oven, placing it on the middle rack. Bake for 20 to 25 minutes, or until the crust is golden brown.

REMOVE FROM THE oven and let sit for 2 minutes before sliding onto a cutting board or pizza peel and using a pizza wheel to slice into eight slices and serve.

Pizza
Planet

Pizza
Planet

RINGS OF SATURN SICILIAN PIZZA

YIELD: 1 PIZZA (4 SERVINGS)

Our ode to the ringed planet is topped with rings of tomatoes and shallots and drizzled with a smooth ricotta drizzle on a thick, airy crust. Plan ahead to make this your dinner time plan—the crust for this takes a bit longer than others.

INGREDIENTS

2 tablespoons olive oil, divided

1 teaspoon cornmeal

1 Focaccia-Style Pizza Dough (page 72)

1 cup (250g) Pizza Planet's Signature Pizza Sauce (page 19)

1 cup (115g) fresh grated Romano cheese

1 cup (4 ounces [115g]) shredded mozzarella cheese

3 plum tomatoes, sliced

2 shallots, sliced

½ cup (115g) ricotta cheese

1 tablespoon heavy cream

½ teaspoon kosher salt

SPREAD 1 TABLESPOON of olive oil on a 9-by-13-inch (23-by-33cm) baking sheet and sprinkle with cornmeal.

STRETCH THE PIZZA dough by hand into a rectangular shape and then place on the baking sheet. Press to stretch the dough to cover the whole pan. Plunge clean fingers into the dough all over and then brush with remaining 1 tablespoon of olive oil. Cover with plastic wrap or a clean kitchen towel and place in a warm, dry place to rise for 1 hour.

ONCE THE RISE time is complete, preheat the oven to 500°F (260°C).

SPREAD THE PIZZA sauce all over the dough. Top with Romano and mozzarella cheeses, plum tomatoes, and shallots. Let sit until the oven is fully heated.

BAKE FOR 20 to 25 minutes, or until the dough is golden at the edges. Remove from the oven.

IN THE BOWL of a blender or mini food processor, combine the ricotta cheese, heavy cream, and salt and blend for 1 to 2 minutes, or until smooth. Drizzle all over the pizza and serve.

Pizza

Focaccia-Style Pizza Dough

YIELD: 1 PIZZA DOUGH

This airy dough is a key component of our Rings of Saturn Sicilian Pizza (page 70) and our Uranus Sicilian Pizza (page 73). The longer rise time (and second rise, as detailed in the individual pizza recipes) gives it a totally unique texture.

INGREDIENTS

1⅓ cups (325ml) lukewarm water

2 teaspoons active dry yeast

3 cups (375g) all-purpose flour

2 tablespoons unsalted butter, melted

1 teaspoon kosher salt

Cooking oil spray

POUR THE WATER into a large bowl. Sprinkle with the yeast and let sit for 4 to 5 minutes, or until the yeast is foamy on top.

ADD THE FLOUR, melted butter, and salt to the bowl and use a rubber spatula to stir to combine. Continue stirring and pressing the dough together with the spatula until elasticky, 3 to 4 minutes.

SPRAY A SECOND large bowl with cooking oil spray. Turn the bowl into the second bowl and cover with a clean kitchen towel. Place in a warm, dry place and allow to rise for 90 minutes.

Note: *If the dough is too sticky to handle, dust with flour before using.*

URANUS SICILIAN PIZZA

YIELD: 1 PIZZA (4 SERVINGS)

Built on a focaccia crust, this pizza is topped with grape tomatoes, red onions, garlic, and herbs as well as Asiago and provolone cheeses. This isn't your ordinary pizza. It's loaded with veggies but also not saucy or cheesy. What's more: It's meant to be served cold, like the ice planet.

INGREDIENTS

2 tablespoons olive oil, divided

1 teaspoon cornmeal

1 Focaccia-Style Pizza Dough (page 72)

2 tablespoons olive oil, divided

1 cup (90g) finely shredded Asiago cheese

1 cup (115g) finely shredded provolone cheese

4 cups (600g) grape tomatoes, halved

½ cup (70g) diced red onions

3 cloves garlic, minced

1 teaspoon dried basil

1 teaspoon dried oregano

LINE A 9-BY-13-INCH (23-by-33cm) baking sheet with parchment paper. Brush with 1 tablespoon of olive oil and sprinkle with cornmeal.

STRETCH THE PIZZA dough by hand into a rectangular shape and then place on the baking sheet. Press to stretch the dough to cover the whole pan. Plunge clean fingers into the dough all over and then brush with 1 tablespoon of olive oil. Cover with plastic wrap or a clean kitchen towel and set in a warm, dry place to rise for 1 hour.

ONCE THE RISE time is complete, preheat the oven to 500°F (260°C).

SPREAD THE ASIAGO and provolone cheeses all over the top. And then cover with grape tomatoes, red onions, minced garlic, basil, and oregano. Let sit until the oven is fully heated.

BAKE FOR 20 to 25 minutes, or until the dough is golden at the edges. Remove from the oven.

SLICE INTO EIGHT pieces and serve.

HOT PIZZA WHEN YOU NEED IT

How to Keep Pizza Warm

If you'd like to keep pizza warm, you'll need an oven heated to the right temperature.

Preheat the oven to 200°F (95°C). Put the pizza on a baking sheet or pizza pan. Slide into the hot oven and bake for up to 1 hour.

Note

If you've been cooking in the oven at 500°F (260°C), you won't also be able to keep the pizza warm in the oven—it will be too hot.

How to Reheat Pizza

Preheat the oven to 500°F (260°C) with a pizza stone set on the rack set to the lowest position. Place the pizza slices directly on the hot pizza stone and cook for 3 to 4 minutes, or until hot. You'll want to watch carefully to ensure the pizza doesn't overcook during this process.

NEPTUNE'S GARLIC SHRIMP PIZZA

YIELD: 1 PIZZA (4 SERVINGS)

Named for the farthest known planet in the solar system, Neptune's Garlic Shrimp Pizza will delight your senses with its complexities. This white pizza is topped with garlic, bright roasted red peppers, fresh herbs, and marinated shrimp along with two cheeses. This pizza is best eaten hot from the oven when all the toppings are at their prime.

INGREDIENTS

1 pound (450g) medium raw shrimp, peeled

1 teaspoon plus 1 tablespoon olive oil, divided

½ teaspoon garlic powder

½ teaspoon onion powder

½ teaspoon paprika

½ teaspoon dried basil

Cooking oil spray

1 teaspoon semolina flour or cornmeal

1 ball Thin Crust Pizza Dough (page 14)

1 cup (4 ounces [115g]) shredded mozzarella cheese

3 cloves garlic, minced

½ cup (85g) thinly sliced roasted red peppers

1 tablespoon minced fresh oregano

1 tablespoon minced fresh basil

½ cup (60g) Romano cheese

Note: *This pizza does not reheat well.*

PREHEAT THE OVEN to 500°F (260°C) with a pizza stone set on the rack at the lowest rung available.

WHILE THE OVEN is heating, in a large bowl, mix together the shrimp, 1 teaspoon of olive oil, the garlic powder, onion powder, paprika, and dried basil. Set aside.

ONCE THE OVEN is heated, begin preparing your pizza. Spray a 16-inch (40cm) round stainless steel pizza pan with cooking oil spray and sprinkle with semolina flour, allowing more to fall toward the center of the pan than the edges.

WITH YOUR HANDS, flatten the pizza dough into a disk. Then let it sit for 1 minute before stretching and turning the dough to form a round, thin crust. Place onto the prepared pizza pan and use your hands to stretch it to the edges and push the dough up the sides of the pan. Once fully stretched, roll the edge of the crust over a little at a time, continuing to work your way around until all the edges have been rolled. Drizzle with the remaining 1 tablespoon of olive oil and use a pastry brush to spread the oil all over, including on the rolled edge of the crust. Prick the dough all over with a fork.

SLIDE THE PAN into the oven, placing it directly on the pizza stone. Bake for 8 minutes.

REMOVE FROM THE oven and spread mozzarella cheese evenly around the crust. Sprinkle with garlic, roasted red peppers, oregano, and basil. Top with the shrimp and Romano cheese.

RETURN TO THE oven on the rack close to the top of the oven and cook for an additional 8 minutes, or until the shrimp are cooked through and the crust is lightly browned.

REMOVE FROM THE oven and let sit for 2 minutes before sliding onto a cutting board or pizza peel and using a pizza wheel to slice into eight slices and serve.

PLUTO: DWARF PLANET PIZZAS

YIELD: 4 PERSONAL-SIZE PIZZAS

One of several dwarf planets in the solar system, Pluto is small but mighty. That's exactly how guests also feel about Dwarf Planet Pizzas, which allow them to customize their pizza experience from our list of toppings. These little pizzas are great for families who all want different toppings.

INGREDIENTS

Cooking oil spray

1 teaspoon semolina flour or cornmeal

1 ball Thin Crust Pizza Dough, divided into 4 pieces

½ cup (125g) Pizza Planet's Signature Pizza Sauce (page 19) or Pesto Sauce (page 20)

1 cup (4 ounces [115g]) shredded mozzarella cheese, divided

2 to 5 choices of toppings (see Buzz Lightyear's Mix-and-Match Toppings on page 80 for some ideas)

SET ONE OVEN rack at the top of the oven and one at the bottom. On the bottom rack, place a pizza stone. Preheat the oven to 500°F (260°C).

ONCE THE OVEN is heated, begin preparing your pizza. Spray a half-sheet stainless steel pizza pan with cooking oil spray and sprinkle with semolina flour, allowing more to fall toward the center of the pan than the edges.

WITH YOUR HANDS and working with one piece of the dough at a time, flatten the pizza dough into a disk. Then let it sit for 1 minute before stretching and turning the dough to form a round, thin crust. It's okay if it's not a perfect circle.

PLACE ONTO THE prepared pizza pan and use your hands to stretch it a little wider. Roll the edge of the crust over a little at a time, continuing to work your way around until all the edges have been rolled. Prick the dough all over with a fork.

SPREAD 2 TABLESPOONS of the sauce onto the pizza and top with ¼ cup (30g) of mozzarella cheese. Sprinkle with desired toppings. Repeat until all the dough has been prepared. (You will either need two baking sheets or to cook these in two batches.)

SLIDE INTO THE oven onto the pizza stone and bake for 10 minutes. Transfer the baking sheet to the top rack and bake for an additional 5 minutes, or until the pizzas are browned at the edges.

REMOVE AND TRANSFER pizzas to four individual plates, using a pizza wheel to slice pizza into four wedges.

Buzz Lightyear's Mix-and-Match Toppings

As Buzz Lightyear says, "To infinity and beyond!" Though in this case, we're talking about the endless options when choosing how to top your own dwarf pizzas. Choose two to five toppings from the list below (recommended: one from the first and second column, plus one to three from the last column) to create your ultimate pizza experience.

PROTEIN

Sausage
Pepperoni
Meatballs
Ham
Bacon
Anchovies
Grilled chicken

VEGGIES

Black olives
Kalamata olives
Roasted red peppers
Bell peppers
Onions
Red onions
Broccoli

HERBS & GARNISHES

Fresh oregano
Fresh basil
Romano cheese
Parmesan cheese
Asiago cheese
Hot honey
Garlic

CHARACTER CALLOUT: BUZZ LIGHTYEAR

Buzz Lightyear is a space ranger sent by Star Command on a mission to protect the galaxy from the evil Emperor Zurg. This star system's greatest superhero has been stationed in the Gamma Quadrant of Sector Four when he finds himself marooned in the strange new land of Andy's Room. Known by his signature white, green, and purple space suit and his catchphrase "To infinity and beyond," Buzz is a master of falling with style.

Pluto Trivia

1. Which object in our solar system was long considered to be a planet and is no longer classified as such?
2. What do we refer to Pluto as now?
3. How far away from the sun is Pluto?
4. How many moons does Pluto have?
5. Pluto is named after the Roman god of _____.

ANSWERS: 1. Pluto, 2. A dwarf planet, 3. 3.7 billion miles, 4. Five, 5. Death

ORBITER MEDITERRANEAN DEEP DISH PIZZA

YIELD: 1 PIZZA (4 SERVINGS)

Pizza Planet's Orbiter Mediterranean Deep Dish Pizza is coming in for a landing at a table near you. This deep dish pizza is layered with cheese, artichokes, kalamata olives, spinach, onions, and tomatoes for a robust veggie pizza experience.

INGREDIENTS

1 Deep Dish Pizza Dough (page 60)

4 cups (1 pound [450g]) shredded mozzarella cheese

2 cups (500g) Pizza Planet's Signature Pizza Sauce (page 19)

4 cups (120g) baby spinach

One 14-ounce (400g) can quartered artichoke hearts, drained

½ cup (85g) sliced roasted red peppers

¼ cup (35g) kalamata olives

1 medium tomato, thinly sliced

¼ cup (30g) grated Parmesan cheese

SPECIAL TOOLS

14-inch (35cm) stainless steel deep dish pizza pan

PREHEAT THE OVEN to 475°F (245°C). Make sure one oven rack is placed in the lower third of the oven and the other placed close to the top.

MEANWHILE, IN A 14-inch (35cm) stainless steel deep dish pizza pan, spread the dough to cover the bottom and creep up the sides to the top. Prick all over with a fork. Cover with a towel and let rise in a warm place for 20 minutes.

SLIDE THE PIZZA pan into the oven and bake for 5 minutes. Remove from the oven.

SPREAD THE CHEESE evenly over the crust. Drizzle the pizza sauce all over, spreading it evenly. Top with the baby spinach, artichoke hearts, roasted red peppers, kalamata olives, and tomato slices. Sprinkle with grated Parmesan cheese.

SLIDE INTO THE oven and bake for 25 minutes. Move the pan to the top rack and cook for an additional 3 to 5 minutes or until golden brown.

REMOVE FROM THE oven and let sit for 5 minutes before cutting into eight slices and serving.

Chapter 4
Interstellar
SIDES AND SALADS

ORBIT GARLIC KNOTS

YIELD: 24 GARLIC KNOTS (6 SERVINGS)

These garlic knots might be little, but they pack a mighty punch with the buttery, garlicky, cheesy flavoring so it's no wonder that customers come in just for these. We think they are perfect for enjoying with all the Pizza Planet pizzas as well as with our salads—but the Orbit Garlic Knots cult following on social media creates all sorts of creative pairings.

The dough will be easiest to work if it's at room temperature. If it's chilled, let it sit on the counter for at least 30 minutes before using.

INGREDIENTS

1 ball Thin Crust Pizza Dough (page 14)

All-purpose flour, for dusting

3 tablespoons unsalted butter

6 cloves garlic, minced

3 tablespoons olive oil

¼ cup (30g) Romano cheese

2 tablespoons fresh minced parsley

⅛ teaspoon crushed red pepper

½ teaspoon kosher salt

PREHEAT THE OVEN to 500°F (260°C) with an oven rack in the lowest position. Place a pizza stone on the lowest rack.

WHILE THE OVEN is heating, put the dough on a floured board and stretch into a large rectangle, about 8 by 12 inches (20 by 30cm). Use a pizza cutter to cut 12 strips, each 1 inch (2.5cm) wide. Then cut the strips in half down the center, creating 24 strips. *(4.1)*

WORKING WITH ONE piece at a time, stretch and roll into a 6-inch (15cm) log. Tie the dough into a knot, carefully tucking the ends beneath the dough. Set aside on the floured board and continue with each dough strip, until all the dough has been tied into knots. *(4.2)*

NOW IT'S TIME to cook. Use tongs to place the knots directly on the hot pizza stone (all 24 should fit) and bake for 6 to 8 minutes or until golden brown.

WHILE THE KNOTS are cooking, in a small saucepan, melt the butter over medium heat. Add the garlic and cook until fragrant, stirring once, about 1 minute. Remove from the heat and pour both the garlic and the butter into a large mixing bowl, using a rubber spatula to get it all. To the garlic butter, add the olive oil, Romano cheese, parsley, red pepper, and salt. Stir vigorously with the rubber spatula to combine.

REMOVE THE COOKED knots from the oven and add them to the mixing bowl. Stir with the rubber spatula as best as you can, then toss to fully coat the knots. Let the bowl sit for 3 minutes and then toss again. Transfer to a serving bowl or plate (don't forget all that garlic butter goodness! Scrape it out!). Serve immediately.

(4.1)

(4.2)

CRATERED (FRIED) MOZZARELLA

YIELD: 12 MOZZARELLA STICKS (4 SERVINGS)

We always say that you haven't had good fried mozzarella until you've had ours. Customers are always asking what's the secret, but that's something we can only share with Pizza Planet Voyagers like you: The double breading gives Pizza Planet's Cratered (Fried) Mozzarella its unforgettable crust. But, please note, these do not reheat well—though that's rarely a problem for anyone. Plan to eat them all.

INGREDIENTS

One 16-ounce (450g) block mozzarella cheese

Note: *You will only use half for this recipe.*

1½ cups (185g) all-purpose flour

1 teaspoon kosher salt

1 teaspoon black pepper

1 teaspoon paprika

1 teaspoon oregano

2 eggs, beaten

1½ cups (150g) Italian breadcrumbs

Canola oil, for frying

Marinara sauce, for serving

FIRST, YOU WILL need to cut the cheese into sticks. To do this, cut from the block of cheese four rectangle pieces each about ½ inch (1.5cm) wide. Cut each, lengthwise, into three pieces.

NOW IT'S TIME to prepare the breading. In a shallow bowl, sift together the flour, salt, pepper, paprika, and oregano. Place the eggs in a second shallow bowl and the breadcrumbs in a third shallow bowl. These should be placed near the stove so you can bread them just before cooking.

PREPARE TO COOK by adding canola oil to a high-sided, flat-bottomed skillet to reach about ½ inch (1.5cm) up the sides of the skillet. Heat over medium-high heat until very hot.

NEXT, BREAD THE mozzarella sticks. To do so, dredge the mozzarella sticks in the flour mixture, then in the egg mixture, and finally in the breadcrumbs. Repeat the process for a second coating.

THEN PLACE THE mozzarella sticks in the pan with the hot oil. Cook for about 3 to 4 minutes or until the bottom side is golden brown. Flip the mozzarella sticks over and cook for an additional 3 to 4 minutes until browned on the bottom as well.

AS THE STICKS complete cooking, remove to a plate. Repeat the process until all the mozzarella has been breaded and cooked.

SERVE IMMEDIATELY, WHILE hot, with marinara sauce.

ROD OF POWER CHEESY BREADSTICKS

YIELD: 12 BREADSTICKS

Speaking of secrets, here's another one: Pizza Planet's signature pizza crust makes the best breadsticks. That's right, we tried a few different doughs for breadsticks but eventually found our pizza dough outperformed them all. Brushed with butter and dusted with a comforting mixture of cheese and garlic, these are great with the Pizza Planet salads. For a spicy version, add 1 teaspoon of diced fresh jalapeño to the butter while it's melting.

INGREDIENTS

1 ball Thin Crust Pizza Dough (page 14)

2 tablespoons unsalted butter, melted

1 teaspoon garlic powder

1 teaspoon dried basil

½ teaspoon kosher salt

2 tablespoons grated Parmesan cheese

Marinara sauce, for serving (optional)

PREHEAT THE OVEN to 425°F (220°C). Line a nonstick baking sheet with parchment paper.

ROLL OUT THE dough to a rectangle, about 8 by 12 inches (20 by 30cm). Cut into 12 strips. *(4.3)*

Tip: *Cut the dough in half down the center, and then cut each half in half. Each quarter should be divided into three even strips.*

WORKING WITH ONE strip of dough at a time, roll until it's 18 inches (45cm) long. Fold the dough in half and then twist. Place on the baking sheet. Continue until all the dough has been used. *(4.4)*

SLIDE THE BAKING sheet into the oven and bake for 15 to 18 minutes or until the breadsticks are golden brown.

BRUSH THE BREADSTICKS with butter as soon as they come out of the oven. *(4.5)*

IN A SMALL bowl, stir together the garlic powder, basil, salt, and cheese. Sprinkle over the breadsticks. Serve immediately, with marinara for dipping, if desired.

PESTO VARIATION: AFTER rolling out the dough in step 2, spread 2 to 3 tablespoons of Pesto Sauce (page 20) evenly over the dough. Proceed with cutting and preparing the breadsticks. This version will be a little messier to work with, but the pesto flavor is worth it.

(4.3)

(4.4)

(4.5)

Toy Story Trivia

1. What does Buzz call his catchphrase button in *Toy Story 4*?
2. Who accidentally gets switched into "Spanish mode" by Rex?
3. What is the name of Sid's dog?
4. Who is Buzz Lightyear's "father"?
5. When Andy goes to college, which toy does he try to bring?

ANSWERS: 1. His inner voice, 2. Buzz Lightyear, 3. Scud, 4. Emperor Zurg, 5. Woody

DWARF GALAXY CALZONES

YIELD: 4 CALZONES

Much like a dwarf galaxy itself, our Dwarf Galaxy Calzones have everything you need in a self-contained package. Filled with three kinds of cheese, along with garlic and herbs, these crust-entombed pizza parlor favorites have a cult following from people who love to request additional fillings. Ham and rosemary is the classic, but almost any pizza topping can make an excellent calzone filling.

INGREDIENTS

All-purpose flour, for dusting

1 ball Thin Crust Pizza Dough (page 14) or Whole Wheat Pizza Dough (page 16), divided into 4 pieces

1 cup (225g) ricotta cheese

1 clove garlic

1 tablespoon fresh oregano

¼ teaspoon salt

¼ teaspoon black pepper

1 cup (4 ounces [115g]) shredded mozzarella cheese

4 tablespoons grated Parmesan cheese

Marinara sauce, for serving

PREHEAT THE OVEN to 500°F (260°C) with a rack set in the center of the oven. Line a large nonstick baking sheet with parchment paper.

ON A FLOURED board, stretch each piece of dough into a very thin round (you may have to do this in batches due to space).

IN THE BOWL of a food processor, combine the ricotta cheese, garlic, oregano, salt, and pepper. Process to smooth, about 2 minutes.

DIVIDE THE RICOTTA mixture evenly among the dough rounds. Top each with ¼ cup (60g) of mozzarella cheese and 1 tablespoon of Parmesan. Fold the dough into a half-moon, pressing to seal the edges. Then roll the edges over to form a rim and press again.

TRANSFER THE HALF-MOON calzones to the prepared baking sheet.

SLIDE THE BAKING sheet into the oven and bake for 12 to 15 minutes, until the tops are browned. Serve with marinara sauce for dipping.

SPACE PORT
STAR

DATE	TABLE	GUESTS	SERVER	ORDER NO.
				112295

ORDER FOR ANDY

Andy Davis is six years old when we meet him in *Toy Story*, and he has a very active and vivid imagination. His favorite toy is Woody, a cowboy. But when Andy's mom gives him a Buzz Lightyear toy, Buzz becomes another favorite. All of Andy's toys, from Bo Peep to Rex to Woody and Buzz, have Andy's name written on the bottom of their feet or shoes.

Andy grows up through the films, playing with his toys less as he becomes a teenager. But even as he heads off to college, he still has a strong connection to them. He gifts his toys to Bonnie so that she can find the joy he found in them, too.

- Jupiter Pie (It's Massive!)
- Cratered (Fried) Mozzarella
- Stardust Cinnamon Twists

DATE	TABLE	GUESTS	SERVER	ORDER NO.
				112295

METEOROID ROASTED MUSHROOM SKEWERS

YIELD: 4 SKEWERS (4 SERVINGS)

Like meteoroids flying into the atmosphere, these roasted mushroom skewers rush to our guests' mouths. Seasoned with rosemary and paprika, the meatiness of these mushrooms and the bold flavor make these a favorite among guests seeking something a little lighter from our menu. Don't forget to suggest them with the next order you take!

INGREDIENTS

Cooking oil spray

One 8-ounce (225g) package whole mushrooms (button or cremini)

2 tablespoons olive oil

1 teaspoon dried rosemary

½ teaspoon paprika

½ teaspoon kosher salt

¼ teaspoon black pepper

PREHEAT THE OVEN to 375°F (190°C). Spray a nonstick baking sheet with cooking oil spray.

IN A MEDIUM bowl, toss the mushrooms with the olive oil, rosemary, paprika, salt, and pepper. Let the mushrooms sit for 5 minutes and toss again, taking care to fully coat the mushrooms with the seasoning mixture.

THREAD FIVE MUSHROOMS onto each skewer. Place the skewers onto the prepared nonstick baking sheet.

SLIDE THE BAKING sheet into the oven and roast for 15 to 20 minutes, turning once, until the mushrooms are a rich brown color. Remove from the oven and serve hot.

Grilling Instructions

Meteoroid Roasted Mushroom Skewers are also great grilled! This alternative version pairs well with any grilled pizza.

IN STEP 3: Use metal skewers for best results. Alternatively, wooden skewers should be soaked in water for at least 30 minutes to prevent burning.

TO COOK: Preheat your grill to medium-high. Place the mushroom skewers on the grates and cook, turning once or twice, for 7 to 8 minutes or until softened and browned all over. Remove carefully from the grill and serve.

Pizza Planet

MISSION CONTROL GARLIC BREAD

YIELD: 1 LOAF GARLIC BREAD (ABOUT 6 SERVINGS)

Mission Control has eyes on all the essential components of space launches. Likewise, with this garlic bread recipe, you'll have control on all the key components. Pizza Planet Voyager: This is important. You must ditch the garlic powder. We are empowering you with our foolproof method for roasting the garlic. It's the roasted garlic, sweet and mellow, that gives this bread its unforgettable flavor.

INGREDIENTS

1 head Roasted Garlic (recipe below)

1 cup (2 sticks [225g]) unsalted butter, softened to room temperature

1 teaspoon kosher salt

1 teaspoon fresh minced parsley

¼ cup (30g) grated Parmesan cheese

PREHEAT THE OVEN to 375°F (190°C). Line a baking sheet with aluminum foil.

CUT THE BREAD down the length and open up. Place on the baking sheet.

IN A LARGE bowl, squeeze all the roasted garlic from the bulb. Add the butter, salt, parsley, and Parmesan and use the tines of a fork to mash together thoroughly.

DIVIDE THE BUTTER mixture evenly among the two bread halves and spread into an even layer with a knife.

SLIDE THE TRAY into the oven and bake for 10 to 15 minutes, or until the butter is melted and the edges of the bread begin to brown.

REMOVE FROM THE oven and let cool for 5 minutes before slicing.

Roasted Garlic

YIELD: 1 HEAD ROASTED GARLIC

INGREDIENTS

1 head garlic

1 tablespoon olive oil

PREHEAT THE OVEN to 400°F (200°C).

CUT OFF THE top ¼ inch (0.5cm) of the garlic head, exposing the cloves. Remove the papery outer layers but leave the head intact.

PLACE THE GARLIC head in the center of a square of aluminum foil. Drizzle the olive oil directly onto the exposed cloves. Wrap the aluminum foil around the garlic head and crimp to seal.

BAKE FOR 40 to 50 minutes, until the cloves are soft and golden brown.

URSA MAJOR BURRATA AND TOMATO BRUSCHETTA

YIELD: 4 SERVINGS

You don't need to look to the north sky to find this constellation. It's available as an appetizer at all Pizza Planet locations. Creamy, cool burrata cheese and a sweet tomato bruschetta are served with crostini, giving guests a change to optimize their own appetizers.

INGREDIENTS

2 cups (340g) cherry tomatoes, quartered

1 teaspoon kosher salt

½ teaspoon ground black pepper

3 tablespoons olive oil

2 cloves garlic, minced

8 large basil leaves, thinly sliced

One 4-ounce (115g) ball burrata

CROSTINI

1 loaf French bread, cut diagonally into slices ¼ inch (0.5cm) thick

1 tablespoon olive oil

PREHEAT THE OVEN to 350°F (180°C).

IN A LARGE bowl, stir together the tomatoes, salt, and pepper. Set aside.

IN A SMALL skillet, heat the oil over medium heat. Add the garlic and cook until fragrant, about 1 minute. Pour the garlic and olive oil mixture into the tomatoes, using a rubber spatula to scrape it all in. Add the basil leaves and toss well. Arrange in a bowl with a spoon. Place the burrata in a second bowl with a spoon, breaking it up a bit for easy use. Allow the tomato and burrata to rest while you make the crostini.

PLACE THE SLICED bread on a baking sheet and brush with olive oil. Slide into the oven and bake for 10 minutes. Transfer the crostini to a serving platter or plate and serve with the tomatoes and burrata.

Note: *Guests should spoon a little tomato and then a little burrata onto their crostini before consuming.*

SUBLUNAR ITALIAN CHOPPED SALAD

YIELD: 4 SALADS (4 SERVINGS)

Our guests report they are in orbit over this Sublunar Italian Chopped Salad. It's a bold mix of cheeses, meat, vegetables, and vinaigrette with so many flavors and textures. The bite of pepperoncini is a good foil for the sweet punch of roasted red peppers. Likewise, the creamy cheeses and zestiness of the red onion are lovely contrasts. If you can't find Castelvetrano olives, use jumbo black olives.

INGREDIENTS

1 head romaine lettuce, washed, dried, and chopped

2 cups (340g) halved cherry tomatoes

1 cup (100g) thinly sliced, chopped red onion

1 cup (115g) cubed provolone cheese (about 4 ounces)

1 cup (115g) cubed salami (about 4 ounces)

1 cup (115g) mozzarella balls

1 cup (140g) pitted Italian Castelvetrano olives

1 cup (140g) thinly sliced roasted red peppers

½ cup (50g) sun-dried tomatoes (packed in oil, but drained)

⅓ cup (50g) thinly sliced pepperoncini peppers

VINAIGRETTE

⅓ cup (80ml) red wine vinegar

¼ cup (60ml) olive oil

½ teaspoon Dijon mustard

1 clove garlic, minced

1 teaspoon honey

1 tablespoon minced fresh oregano

½ teaspoon kosher salt

¼ teaspoon ground black pepper

IN A VERY large bowl, combine the lettuce, tomatoes, red onion, provolone cheese, salami, mozzarella, olives, roasted red peppers, sun-dried tomatoes, and pepperoncini peppers. Toss well to combine.

IN A SMALL bowl, whisk together the red wine vinegar, olive oil, Dijon mustard, garlic, honey, oregano, salt, and black pepper. Whisk to combine. Pour over the salad and toss well.

DIVIDE THE SALAD evenly between four bowls or plates. Serve.

COSMIC LOADED CHICKEN CAESAR BOWL

YIELD: 4 SALADS (4 SERVINGS)

Pizza Planet guests say that it's a bold new world with this cosmic twist on a classic. The galaxy will rejoice when they try this upgraded classic, a chicken Caesar salad blasting off with piles of juicy tomatoes, zesty red onions, creamy avocado, and salty bacon. And remember: Guests can always enjoy this with a side of Orbit Garlic Knots (page 86) or Rod of Power Cheesy Breadsticks (page 90) if they want an even bigger cosmic upgrade.

INGREDIENTS

GRILLED CHICKEN

1 pound (450g) boneless, skinless chicken breast

½ cup (120ml) Caesar dressing

SALAD

4 cups (200g) romaine lettuce

½ cup (60g) freshly grated Romano cheese

⅔ cup (160ml) Caesar dressing

1 cup (30g) croutons

1 cup (170g) cherry tomatoes

½ cup (70g) diced red onions

2 avocados, diced

½ pound (225g) bacon, prepared

4 hard-boiled eggs, chopped

IN AN AIRTIGHT container, combine the chicken breast and the ½ cup (120ml) of Caesar dressing. Seal and let marinate in the fridge for 1 hour.

PREPARE YOUR GRILL for cooking, heating it to medium heat. Place the chicken breasts on the grill and cook for 5 to 7 minutes per side, or until cooked through. Thicker chicken breasts may need to cook longer. Remove from the grill and let rest for 10 minutes before slicing.

IN A LARGE bowl, toss together the lettuce, Romano cheese, Caesar dressing, and croutons. Divide evenly among four plates, piling the salad onto the plates. Top each of the four salads with a quarter of the sliced chicken breast, the cherry tomatoes, red onions, avocado, bacon, and hard-boiled eggs, arranging the toppings in piles around the lettuce. Serve immediately, encouraging guests to toss their salad ingredients together before consuming.

OUTER SPACE GREEK SALAD

YIELD: 4 SALADS (4 SERVINGS)

Have a customer seeking a salad that's far out? Then Outer Space Greek Salad might just be the perfect option. Filled with juicy tomatoes, cool cucumbers, crisp green peppers, salty feta, briny kalamata olives, and zesty red onion and finished with a tart lemon vinaigrette, this bold Greek salad is a perfect pairing for all the pizzas in the Pizza Planet repertoire.

INGREDIENTS

4 cups (200g) romaine lettuce, chopped

2 tomatoes, diced

1 cucumber, peeled and diced

1 green bell pepper, cored and diced

4 ounces (115g) feta cheese, crumbled

½ cup (70g) kalamata olives

¼ cup (35g) diced red onion

¼ cup (60ml) olive oil

1 lemon, juiced and zested (about ¼ cup [60ml] juice)

½ teaspoon kosher salt

½ teaspoon black pepper

IN A LARGE mixing bowl, toss together the romaine, tomatoes, cucumber, green pepper, feta, kalamata olives, and red onion until the ingredients are well distributed.

IN A SMALL bowl, whisk together the olive oil, lemon juice, lemon zest, salt, and pepper. This should render the lemon vinaigrette cloudy in appearance as the olive oil emulsifies. Taste the vinaigrette and adjust the seasonings as desired.

ADD THE DRESSING to the salad and toss thoroughly to combine. The vinaigrette should be evenly distributed through the ingredients before you divide the salad among four plates or bowls. Serve immediately.

Tip: *Have a guest who likes it hotter? Add a whole pepperoncini pepper or two to each plate just before serving. It's a spectral flavor experience!*

Pizza Planet

Chapter 5
Starry SWEETS AND SIPS

GALACTIC BROWNIES

YIELD: 12 BROWNIES

Chocolate fans, rejoice! Pizza Planet's Galactic Brownies are a gooey, chocolatey, out-of-this-world way to end your favorite meal. Fudgy brownies are topped with a layer of smooth chocolate ganache and sprinkles arranged in galactic swirls. Some guests love to order these served with a scoop of vanilla or chocolate ice cream.

INGREDIENTS

¼ cup (4 tablespoons [60g]) unsalted butter

2 ounces (60g) semisweet chocolate, broken into pieces

¾ cup (155g) packed light brown sugar

2 large eggs

1 teaspoon vanilla extract

½ cup (60g) all-purpose flour

1½ teaspoons instant coffee

Pinch kosher salt

CHOCOLATE GANACHE

¼ cup (60ml) heavy cream

4 ounces (115g) semisweet chocolate

Sprinkles such as stars, silver and gold disks, and dark blue, dark green, and white nonpareils

PREHEAT THE OVEN to 375°F (190°C). Grease an 8-inch (20cm) square glass baking pan with cooking oil spray. Set aside.

IN A SMALL saucepan, melt the butter and chocolate together over medium heat, stirring constantly until completely melted and combined. Remove from the heat. Let sit for 5 minutes.

IN A LARGE mixing bowl, whisk together the brown sugar and eggs. Drizzle the chocolate-butter mixture, whisking constantly, into the brown sugar mixture until fully combined. Whisk in the vanilla.

IN A SMALL bowl, sift together the flour, instant coffee, and salt. Add to the chocolate mixture and whisk well until combined.

POUR THE BATTER into the prepared baking pan.

BAKE FOR 20 to 25 minutes, until cooked through. Use a toothpick inserted in the center to determine: If it comes out clean, the brownies are done.

LET COOL COMPLETELY before adding ganache.

ONCE THE BROWNIES are cooled, make the ganache. In a small saucepan, combine the heavy cream and chocolate over medium heat. Stir constantly until the chocolate is fully melted. Remove from the heat and whisk the heavy cream and chocolate. Let sit for 10 minutes before pouring onto the brownies. You'll want to decorate with sprinkles while the ganache is still soft. Use the sprinkles to create swirls and lines, creating a galaxy effect.

ALLOW THE BROWNIES to sit for at least 1 hour before slicing, or until the ganache has set. Use a knife to cut into a 4-by-3 grid, creating 12 brownies.

FLYING SAUCER GIANT CHOCOLATE CHIP COOKIES

YIELD: 14 LARGE COOKIES

These oversize cookies are hot sellers at our Pizza Planet locations. Some of our guests even order them to go after a meal! Keep them handy and see how they lift off with guests like flying saucers from another world. You'll need a large cookie scoop with a 3-tablespoon capacity for these. If you have a classic ice-cream scoop, that will work as well.

INGREDIENTS

1 cup (2 sticks [225g]) unsalted butter, softened

¾ cup (150g) granulated sugar

¾ cup (155g) packed light brown sugar

2 teaspoons vanilla extract

2 large eggs

2¼ cups (280g) all-purpose flour

2 teaspoons baking powder

1 teaspoon kosher salt, plus more for sprinkling

2 cups (340g) milk chocolate chips

PREHEAT THE OVEN to 375°F (190°C) with a rack positioned just above the center of the oven. Line a baking sheet with parchment paper. Set aside. Because these cookies spread a lot with baking, it's recommended to cook these in two or three batches for optimal baking and so the cookies have enough room.

IN THE BOWL of a stand mixer fitted with the paddle attachment, beat the butter until light and fluffy, 2 to 3 minutes. Add the sugars and vanilla and beat well until combined, about 2 minutes. Add the eggs one at a time, beating well after each addition.

IN A LARGE bowl, sift together the flour, baking powder, and salt. With the mixer running on its lowest setting, add the flour mixture a little at a time to the butter mixture, until all is just incorporated.

STIR IN THE chocolate chips.

USE A LARGE cookie scoop (3-tablespoon capacity), to scoop out balls of dough onto the prepared cookie sheet, leaving at least 3 inches (7.5cm) between each cookie. Bake for 15 to 18 minutes, or until golden at the edges and cooked through. The center of the cookie shouldn't look moist.

REMOVE FROM THE oven and let sit for 5 minutes before transferring to a cooling rack. Repeat until all dough has been used. For best results, the cookie sheet should be cooled when the next batch is placed on it.

COOKIES CAN BE eaten immediately or stored in an airtight container for up to 5 days.

TRANSLUNAR PEANUT BUTTER PIE

YIELD: 1 PIE (8 SERVINGS)

Slices of Pizza Planet's Translunar Peanut Butter Pie will send you to the moon with joy. The creamy peanut butter pie is topped with bits of chocolate and peanut, giving a touch of flavor and texture variation. A tip for cutting: Clean your knife between cuts for presentation-ready slices.

INGREDIENTS

GRAHAM CRACKER CRUST

Cooking oil spray

12 graham cracker sheets

2 tablespoons packed brown sugar

½ teaspoon kosher salt

6 tablespoons (90g) unsalted butter, melted

FILLING

1 cup (240ml) heavy cream

8 ounces (225g) cream cheese, softened to room temperature

1 cup (280g) creamy peanut butter

⅔ cup (75g) powdered sugar

1 teaspoon vanilla extract

TOPPING

2 tablespoons mini chocolate chips

2 tablespoons chopped honey roasted peanuts

PREHEAT THE OVEN to 350°F (180°C). Spray a pie plate with cooking oil spray and set aside.

IN A FOOD processor, break apart the graham cracker sheets and add the brown sugar and salt. Process until the crumbs are uniformly fine. With the processor running on medium, drizzle in the butter, continuing to process for 1 minute after all the butter has been added.

POUR THE CRACKER crumbs into the prepared pie plate. Press with a flat-bottomed object (such as a ramekin) to create one even layer all over the bottom and up the sides of the plate.

SLIDE INTO THE oven and bake for 10 minutes, or until beginning to brown at the edges. Remove from the oven and let cool for 10 minutes away from the stove.

IN THE BOWL of a stand mixer fitted with the whisk attachment, beat the heavy cream to stiff peaks at medium to medium-high speed. This will take 4 to 6 minutes. Scrape the whipped cream into a bowl and set aside.

INTO THE STAND mixer bowl, combine the cream cheese, peanut butter, powdered sugar, and vanilla. Using the whisk attachment (no need to clean between steps—it's all combining in the end!), whisk until fluffy, 3 to 5 minutes. You'll want to scrape down the sides of the bowl a couple of times to ensure uniform fluffiness.

REMOVE THE BOWL from the stand mixer and tap the whisk to ensure all the peanut butter mixture is in the bowl. Add the whipped heavy cream and fold together with a rubber spatula.

POUR THE PEANUT butter mixture into the prepared piecrust. Sprinkle all over with the mini chocolate chips and honey roasted peanuts. Place in the fridge and chill for at least 2 hours before serving.

CRUST ALTERNATIVES

Peanut Butter Pie is delightful with an array of crusts. The following alternatives can be substituted for the graham crackers to create a whole new flavor experience. Use about 1½ cups (120g) lightly crushed cookies or crackers to equal the 12 graham cracker sheets:

- Chocolate graham crackers
- Ginger snap cookies
- Vanilla wafer cookies

TOPPING ALTERNATIVE

Chocolate Ganache

Looking for a more chocolatey pie? Substitute the mini chocolate chips with a smooth chocolate ganache before chilling the pie.

INGREDIENTS

¼ cup (60ml) heavy cream

4 ounces (115g) semisweet chocolate

IN A SMALL saucepan, combine the heavy cream and chocolate over medium heat. Stir constantly until the chocolate is fully melted. Remove from the heat and whisk the heavy cream and chocolate. Let sit for 10 minutes before pouring onto the pie. Top with chopped peanuts.

Toy Story Trivia

1. What's the name of the toy store in *Toy Story 2*?
2. Which toy guards Sunnyside Daycare using the hall cameras?
3. What does the badge on Woody's vest say?
4. How do the toys cross the busy intersection in *Toy Story 2*?
5. What is the blue wallpaper in Andy's room dotted with?
6. What is Rex's favorite video game?
7. Which toy tries to steal Woody's voice box?
8. What is the name of Woody's horse?
9. Who does Buzz Lightyear work for?
10. What are the names of Bo's sheep?

ANSWERS: 1. Al's Toy Barn, 2. The Monkey, 3. Sheriff, 4. Using traffic cones, 5. Clouds, 6. Buzz Lightyear: Attack on Zurg, 7. Gabby Gabby, 8. Bullseye, 9. Star Command, 10. Billy, Goat, and Gruff

STARDUST CINNAMON TWISTS

YIELD: 12 TWISTS (4 SERVINGS)

The stars aligned! Grab one of these crispy, flaky Stardust Cinnamon Twists and plunge them into the unforgettable Chocolate Hazelnut Dip for the ultimate end to your Pizza Planet adventure.

INGREDIENTS

All-purpose flour, for dusting

1 sheet puff pastry, defrosted

2 tablespoons unsalted butter, melted

2 tablespoons light brown sugar

1 teaspoon cinnamon

CHOCOLATE HAZELNUT DIP

3 tablespoons heavy cream

½ cup (140g) chocolate hazelnut spread

⅛ teaspoon kosher salt

PREHEAT THE OVEN to 400°F (200°C). Line a baking sheet with parchment paper.

ON A FLOURED board, lay out the thawed puff pastry. Brush one side with butter. In a small bowl, combine the brown sugar and cinnamon and then sprinkle all over the butter side of the dough.

FOLD THE DOUGH in half. Use a pizza wheel or a sharp knife to cut the dough into 12 strips.

WORKING WITH ONE at a time, twist the strip and place on the prepared baking sheet. Leave space between the twists, as they will puff upon baking.

SLIDE INTO THE oven and bake for 14 to 16 minutes, or until golden.

IN A SMALL saucepan, heat the heavy cream, chocolate hazelnut spread, and salt over medium-low heat, stirring constantly until smooth. This will take 2 to 3 minutes. Remove from the heat and pour into a small bowl.

SERVE THE TWISTS and dip immediately.

BLACK HOLE DARK CHOCOLATE MOUSSE

YIELD: 4 SERVINGS

Step into the void with time-stopping Black Hole Dark Chocolate Mousse. One bite will have guests pausing everything else just to enjoy. Creamy, chocolatey, and airy, this mousse is a decadent way to end a meal. Leftovers can be taken to go and stored uncovered in the fridge for up to three days—if they last that long.

INGREDIENTS

4 ounces (115g) semisweet chocolate

½ cup (120ml) heavy cream

½ teaspoon vanilla extract

2 large pasteurized eggs, separated

¼ teaspoon kosher salt

½ teaspoon instant coffee

2 tablespoons granulated sugar

Whipped cream, for serving (optional)

IN A SMALL saucepan, heat the chocolate and the heavy cream over medium heat, stirring constantly until the chocolate is melted. Remove from the heat and let cool for 5 minutes.

IN A LARGE bowl, whisk together the vanilla and egg yolks until smooth. Drizzle the chocolate mixture in, whisking constantly, until all the chocolate has been added, and continue whisking for 2 minutes. The mixture will expand slightly with the whisking.

IN THE BOWL of a stand mixer fitted with the whisk attachment, combine the egg whites, salt, coffee, and sugar. Beat with the mixer running on medium until stiff peaks form, 3 to 4 minutes.

ADD A THIRD of the egg white mixture to the chocolate mixture and fold to combine. Add the remaining egg white mixture and again fold to combine.

DIVIDE THE CHOCOLATE mousse evenly among four bowls and chill for at least 2 hours before serving.

SATELLITE FRUIT TART SUNDAES

YIELD: 12 TARTS

Guests love to end their meal on a cool note with these Satellite Fruit Tart Sundaes. Buttery cookie shells are topped with a scoop of vanilla ice cream and finished off with our sweet berry topping. We recommend providing whipped cream for an even sweeter finish. Though the cookie shells can be made up to four days in advance and stored in an airtight container, they are best on the day they're made.

INGREDIENTS

TART SHELLS

Cooking oil spray

1 cup (115g) all-purpose flour

½ teaspoon salt

¼ teaspoon baking powder

½ cup (1 stick [115g]) unsalted butter, softened

¾ cup (150g) granulated sugar

1 teaspoon vanilla extract

1 large egg

SUNDAE TOPPINGS

1 cup (150g) fresh strawberries, halved

⅓ cup (40g) fresh raspberries

⅓ cup (50g) fresh blueberries

⅓ cup (40g) fresh blackberries

1 tablespoon apricot jam

1½ cups (225g) vanilla ice cream

TO MAKE THE TART SHELLS

MAKE SURE THE oven rack is in the center of the oven and preheat to 375°F (190°C). Spray 12 muffin cups with cooking oil spray.

IN A MEDIUM bowl, sift together flour, salt, and baking powder.

IN THE BOWL of a stand mixer fitted with the paddle attachment, beat the butter on medium until it's smooth. Add the sugar and vanilla. Beat until fully incorporated, about 2 minutes. Add the egg and beat for about another minute, until well combined.

WITH THE MIXER running on its lowest setting, add the flour mixture a little at a time. Don't overblend—you want it just combined, and it should only take a few seconds per addition.

USE A MEDIUM cookie scoop to place rounded tablespoonfuls of the dough into the muffin tin cavities, dividing it equally among them. Press gently into the muffin tin cavities to encourage the shells to crater while baking.

SLIDE THE MUFFIN tin into the oven and cook for 12 to 15 minutes or until the edges of the cookie tart shells are just beginning to brown. The cookie should appear cooked throughout (no moist center).

REMOVE FROM THE oven and place the muffin tin on a cooling rack and cool for 10 minutes. Loosen the edges of the tart shells with a knife and turn out onto the rack. Cool completely.

TO ASSEMBLE THE SUNDAES

COMBINE THE FRUIT in a medium bowl, stirring well to distribute.

PLACE THE APRICOT jam in a small microwave-safe bowl and microwave for 30 seconds. It should be warm and liquidy. Add to the fruit and toss to combine. Use immediately or chill for up to 24 hours before using.

PLACE A TART shell on a plate and top with a generous scoop of ice cream, placing it on top of the shell. Spoon the fruit onto the ice cream, taking care to place it in an artful pattern. Serve immediately.

TOPPING ADDITIONS

ADDING A TEASPOON or so of the following toppings can make these sundaes even more delightful. A dollop of whipped cream is also a good idea!

- Sprinkles
- Mini chocolate chips
- Chopped peanuts
- Sliced almonds
- Shredded coconut
- Granola

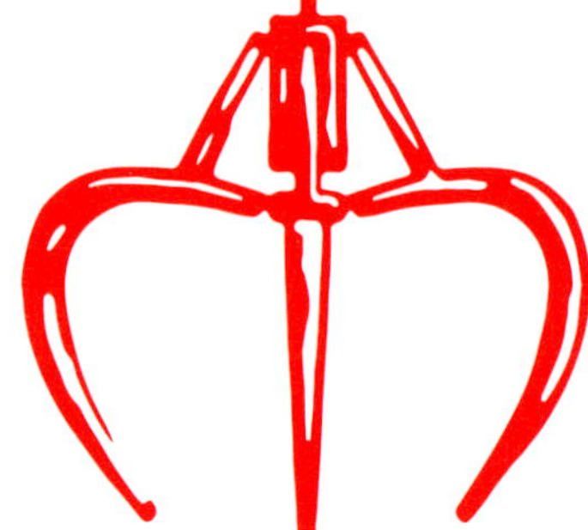

DATE	TABLE	GUESTS	SERVER	ORDER NO.
				161602

ORDER FOR BONNIE

Bonnie is a friendly, shy, playful little girl who becomes the new owner of Woody, Buzz, Jessie, and all of Andy's toys when he heads off to college. She wears colorful, layered outfits and attends Sunnyside Daycare, where her mom works. That's where she first meets Woody.

Bonnie's mom and Andy's mom are friends. When Andy comes to give her his toys, Bonnie is excited to find Woody in the box. But Andy hesitates to give him away, until he sees that she lights up around Woody, too.

- Venus-Style (Inside-Out) Pizza
- Cosmic Loaded Chicken Caesar Bowl
- Satellite Fruit Tart Sundaes

DATE	TABLE	GUESTS	SERVER	ORDER NO.
				161602

ASTEROID BELT COOKIES AND CREAM CHEESECAKE

YIELD: 1 CHEESECAKE (ABOUT 9 SERVINGS)

Guests will feel like they flew into an asteroid belt when they bite into this creamy, chocolatey Cookies and Cream Cheesecake. But no need to dodge these space rocks though! A sweet chocolate crust made with chocolate sandwich cookies is topped with our light and airy cheesecake dotted with more chocolate sandwich cookies. It's creamy. It's chocolatey. It's divine. And it makes a supreme end to any Pizza Planet meal!

INGREDIENTS

CRUST

Cooking oil spray

12 chocolate sandwich cookies

¼ cup (60g) unsalted butter, melted

CHEESECAKE

One 8-ounce (225g) bar cream cheese, softened to room temperature

½ cup (100g) granulated sugar

1 teaspoon vanilla extract

1 cup (240ml) heavy cream

12 chocolate sandwich cookies, crushed, plus 4 lightly crushed cookies for garnish

HEAT OVEN TO 400°F (200°C). Spray an 8-inch (20cm) square glass baking pan with cooking oil spray.

IN THE BOWL of a food processor, pulse the chocolate sandwich cookies for the crust until pulverized. With the food processor running on low, drizzle the butter in until fully combined.

PRESS THE CHOCOLATE sandwich-cookie crumbs into the bottom of the prepared baking pan, pressing into a single layer with a flat-bottomed container such as a ramekin.

SLIDE INTO THE oven and bake for 10 minutes. The crust may be bubbling when you remove it from the oven. This is good. Let it sit and cool for at least 15 minutes before filling.

TO MAKE THE cheesecake filling, in the bowl of a stand mixer fitted with the whisk attachment, combine the cream cheese, sugar, and vanilla. Beat together until smooth, about 2 minutes. Add the heavy cream and run the mixer on low for 1 minute. Increase the speed to medium and whisk for 2 to 3 minutes, until thick and smooth. Stir in the 12 crushed chocolate sandwich cookies.

TRANSFER THE CREAM cheese mixture to the baking dish with the chocolate sandwich-cookie crust. Garnish with the four lightly crushed chocolate sandwich cookies.

CHILL FOR AT least 2 hours before serving.

SPACECRAFT DESSERT PIZZA

YIELD: 1 DESSERT PIZZA

Here comes the sweetest spacecraft in the universe! Spacecraft Dessert Pizza features a creamy, rich layer of chocolate hazelnut spread with mellow bananas and a sprinkle of cosmic dust—aka powdered sugar. What a sweet way to end a meal!

INGREDIENTS

Cooking oil spray

1 teaspoon semolina flour or cornmeal

½ ball pizza dough

2 tablespoons chocolate hazelnut spread

1 banana, thinly sliced

1 teaspoon powdered sugar

PREHEAT THE OVEN to 500°F (260°C) with a pizza stone set on the rack at the lowest rung available.

ONCE THE OVEN is heated, begin preparing your pizza. Line a 16-inch (40cm) round stainless-steel pizza pan with parchment paper, spray with cooking oil spray, and sprinkle with semolina flour, allowing more to fall toward the center of the pan than the edges.

WITH YOUR HANDS, flatten the pizza dough into a disk. Then let it sit for 1 minute before stretching and turning the dough to form a round, thin crust. Place onto the prepared pizza pan and use your hands to stretch it into a circle (it won't fill the pan). Once stretched, roll the edge of the crust over a little at a time, continuing to work your way around until all the edges have been rolled. Prick the dough all over with a fork.

SLIDE THE PAN into the oven, placing it directly on the pizza stone. Bake for 8 to 10 minutes, or until golden brown.

REMOVE FROM THE oven and spread with chocolate hazelnut spread immediately. Let sit for 1 minute and then spread more. The chocolate hazelnut spread will soften with the heat.

ARRANGE THE BANANA slices on top, then dust with powdered sugar. Slice with a pizza wheel and serve.

CELESTIAL VANILLA BLUEBERRY CUPCAKES

YIELD: 12 CUPCAKES

Our lightest, airiest cupcakes! Planetary Vanilla Blueberry Cupcakes are dotted with tart berries and topped with our sweet made-in-house vanilla buttercream frosting. (Yes, that means you are making the frosting.) If desired, garnish these with additional blueberries.

INGREDIENTS

CUPCAKES

1 cup (115g) all-purpose flour

½ cup (100g) granulated sugar

1 teaspoon baking soda

1 teaspoon baking powder

½ teaspoon salt

1 large egg

½ cup (120ml) milk

¼ cup (60ml) canola oil

1 teaspoon vanilla extract

1 cup (140g) fresh blueberries

FROSTING

½ cup (115g [1 stick]) unsalted butter

2 cups (230g) powdered sugar

3 tablespoons heavy cream

1 teaspoon vanilla extract

PREHEAT THE OVEN to 375°F (190°C). Line 12 muffin cups with cupcake liners.

IN A LARGE bowl, sift together the flour, sugar, baking soda, baking powder, and salt. Add the egg, milk, oil, and vanilla and stir until smooth, about 2 minutes. Stir in the blueberries.

DIVIDE THE BATTER evenly among the cupcake liners. Bake for 18 to 20 minutes, until a toothpick inserted in the center comes out clean. Remove from the oven and let cool thoroughly.

ONCE THE CUPCAKES are cooled, it's time to make the frosting. In the bowl of a stand mixer fitted with the whisk attachment, combine the butter, powdered sugar, heavy cream, and vanilla. Beat for 2 to 3 minutes, first on low then increasing the speed to medium, or until smooth and fluffy. Pipe onto the cupcakes.

LOCAL STAR CLUSTER BLUEBERRY MINT ICED TEA

YIELD: 4 SERVINGS

Refreshing and fruity, Local Star Cluster Blueberry Mint Iced Tea is a table order favorite! (As noted on the menu, it is available by the glass or pitcher.) There's no need to make this before every shift. Leftovers will store well in the refrigerator for up to five days.

INGREDIENTS

6 cups (1.4L) water, divided

⅓ cup (70g) sugar

½ cup (70g) fresh blueberries

3 peppermint tea bags

3 chamomile tea bags

1 tablespoon lemon juice

IN A SMALL saucepan, heat 1 cup (200ml) of water, the sugar, and blueberries over medium heat. Stirring constantly, cook for 8 to 10 minutes or until the sugar is incorporated and the blueberries pop. Remove from the heat and strain the mixture into a pitcher, pressing the blueberries against the mesh of the strainer to extract the maximum blueberry flavor. Discard the remaining blueberry skins and flesh in the strainer.

HEAT THE REMAINING 5 cups (1.2L) of water to boiling. Remove from the heat and add the tea bags. Steep for 5 minutes. Remove the tea bags and let cool for 10 minutes.

ADD THE TEA to the pitcher along with the lemon juice. Stir well. Chill in the fridge for at least 1 hour before serving over ice.

PIZZA PLANET MEGA GULP FROZEN STRAWBERRY LEMONADE

YIELD: 4 SERVINGS

Frosty and refreshing, this is the interplanetary drink many of our youngest customers come back for time and again! Sweet-tart lemonade with strawberry flair for all your sipping needs! The strawberry lemonade mixture can be made and refrigerated for up to five days. Just blend in the ice when it's time to make a serving.

INGREDIENTS

3 cups (700ml) water, divided

¾ cup (150g) sugar

¾ cup (180ml) freshly squeezed lemons, juiced (about 4 lemons)

3 cups (1 pound [450g]) frozen strawberries

Ice (optional)

IN A SMALL saucepan, combine ¾ cup (180ml) of water and the sugar. Heat over medium heat, stirring constantly, until the sugar dissolves. Remove from the heat and let cool for at least 10 minutes.

IN A BLENDER, combine the simple syrup, the remaining 2¼ cups (520ml) of water, the lemon juice, and frozen strawberries. Blend until fully combined.

SERVE AS IS or blend with additional ice to make it even slushier.

Pizza
Planet
Pizza
Planet

PINEAPPLE ORANGE SUNBEAM

YIELD: 1 SERVING

As bright as it sounds, the Pineapple Orange Sunbeam is a refreshing sipper that pairs well with the classic pizzas. We recommend using all chilled ingredients for the best sipping experience. This can also be made as a slushie.

INGREDIENTS

1 cup (225g) ice

½ cup (120ml) pineapple juice

½ cup (120ml) orange juice

¼ teaspoon vanilla extract

¼ cup (60ml) club soda

1 teaspoon grenadine

IN A TALL glass, combine the ice, pineapple juice, orange juice, and vanilla. Stir. Pour in the club soda and drizzle in the grenadine. Serve.

MAKE IT A slushie: In a blender, combine the ice, pineapple juice, orange juice, and vanilla, adding more ice as desired. Blend until uniformly icy. Transfer to a glass and top with club soda and grenadine.

MILKY WAY WHITE HOT CHOCOLATE

YIELD: 1 SERVING

Creamy as the Milky Way, this white hot chocolate is a sweet treat. This drink can be doubled, tripled, or quadrupled for more guests. But don't make more than you need at the time. The variations are a popular way for guests to customize their drinks.

INGREDIENTS

1 cup (240ml) milk

¼ cup (35g) chopped white chocolate

¼ teaspoon vanilla extract

IN A SMALL saucepan, combine the milk, white chocolate, and vanilla over medium heat. Stir constantly until the chocolate is melted. Remove from the heat. Serve.

HOT CHOCOLATE VARIATIONS

PEPPERMINT WHITE HOT CHOCOLATE

Add ⅛ teaspoon of peppermint extract to the milk mixture while heating. Top with whipped cream and crushed peppermint candy.

RASPBERRY WHITE HOT CHOCOLATE

Add 1 teaspoon of raspberry syrup to the drink just before serving. Stir to combine.

DOUBLE CHOCOLATE WHITE HOT CHOCOLATE

After pouring the white hot chocolate into a mug, top with whipped cream and shards of dark chocolate.

About the Author

For more than two decades, Sarah Walker Caron has been writing about food for websites, magazines, newspapers, news sites, and books. Now the author of ten books, including *Harry Potter and Fantastic Beasts: Official Wizarding World Cookbook*, *Classic Diners of Maine*, and *The Super Easy 5-Ingredient Cookbook*, she specializes in quick and easy cooking from scratch and aims to encourage home cooks to get into the kitchen more.

In 2005, she founded *Sarah's Cucina Bella* (sarahscucinabella.com) to begin her food writing journey. No one is more surprised than her that it's still going more than twenty years later, but she loves her readers and sharing her recipes.

In addition to food writing, Sarah teaches journalism at the University of Maine and Husson University. She's also a Pushcart-nominated essayist, former newspaper editor, and longtime freelance writer. Her work has appeared in dozens of outlets including SheKnows, Betty Crocker, Tablespoon, and *Fine Cooking*.

Acknowledgments

Writing a cookbook is a special undertaking that requires precision, patience, and lots of recipe testing. Thank you to my daughter, Paige Caron, for enduring so many weeks of pizza making and eating, offering unvarnished input on every recipe in this book. Thank you also to Rowen Osmer, who became an unexpected and much appreciated taste tester of recipes in this book, as well as Paige's entire Humanities class at Bangor High.

Thanks also to Gibran Graham, who declared the Cleared to Enter Barbecue Chicken Pizza one of the best ever. It is the tastebuds of many that ensure these recipes hit just right.

Thank you goes to my son, Will Caron, for listening to me talk about pizza and other recipes on phone call after phone call. Thank you also to my family for their love and support of all my endeavors, and for eating that first test pizza. And thanks to friends Julia Bayly, Melissa Gerety, and Angelmary Koola for your support.

Everyone needs an editor, and I am so grateful to mine, Thom O'Hearn, who has been a champion of this book every step of the way. I couldn't have done this without him.

And finally, thanks to Tony Ronzio whose early intergalactic brainstorming helped me blast off into creating the outline that became this book.

FRESHEST
IN THE
GALAXY

Index

N

O

P

PO Box 3088
San Rafael, CA 94912
www.insighteditions.com

Find us on Facebook: www.facebook.com/InsightEditions
Follow us on Instagram: @insighteditions

ISBN: 979-8-3374-0222-2

Publisher: Raoul Goff
SVP, Group Publisher: Vanessa Lopez
VP, Creative: Chrissy Kwasnik
VP, Manufacturing: Alix Nicholaeff
Editorial Director: Thom O'Hearn
Art Director: Stuart Smith
Managing Editor: Shannon Ballesteros
Production Manager: Deena Hashem
Strategic Production Planner: Lina s Palma-Temena

Interior Design: Emily Austin, The Sly Studio
Page Layout: Teddie Sheldon, The Sly Studio

Photography by Carla Choy

Insight Editions, in association with Roots of Peace, will plant two trees for each tree used in the manufacturing of this book. Roots of Peace is an internationally renowned humanitarian organization dedicated to eradicating land mines worldwide and converting war-torn lands into productive farms and wildlife habitats. Roots of Peace will plant two million fruit and nut trees in Afghanistan and provide farmers there with the skills and support necessary for sustainable land use.

Manufactured in China by Insight Editions

10 9 8 7 6 5 4 3 2 1

Pizza Planet

Pizza Planet